M000282678

Several of us say about Dr. Perkins, "no hi[...]
call from him out of the blue is always a bl[...]
pulling at him, he makes room to build fri[...]
easy to hear him broach this subject becau[...]
will be yet another legacy work of this great legend and all that Jesus has placed in him
to call the body to walk in being bound together.

**ERIC M. MASON**
Author of *Woke Church* and pastor of Epiphany Fellowship in Philadelphia, PA

At the heart of John and Vera Mae Perkins's ministry of evangelism, witness for
justice, and reconciliation has been the uncanny and surprising ability to draw people
from all generations, walks of life, and backgrounds into their circle of friendship.
Over the years, they have built a global community of friends who have themselves
responded to the high calling to be friends of Jesus, living out the principles of
relocation, reconciliation, and redistribution that are at the heart of a tough, enduring
gospel powerful enough to transform the most desperate human situations in
their neighborhoods and cities. Terry and I, as twenty-year-old newlyweds, had the
trajectory of our lives changed forever by friendship with the Perkins.

**H. SPEES**
Senior Associate at Leadership Foundations; Director of Strategic Initiatives for City
of Fresno

John Perkins and I met in Vicksburg, in 1973. We each had a burden to bring healing
and help to at-risk communities. It did not take long for us to realize that we were
kindred spirits. Over these years, many of his friends have become my friends and our
relationship has opened doors in surprising ways. As a Dutch Calvinist, I have always
been part of a somewhat isolated part of the broader evangelical community, but if
I mention that I am a friend of John Perkins, I suddenly become acceptable. It is as
though I have a merit badge that announces that I am OK. John Perkins enfleshes the
very message of this book. And I am privileged and grateful to be among those he calls
friend.

**GARY VANDERARK**
Professor of Neurosurgery University of Colorado

For years Dr. John Perkins has been an inspiration to me and has helped fuel my
passion for racial reconciliation and multicultural ministry. To see his dream and
mine realized in the multiracial church I pastor will inspire generations to come. Dr.
Perkins's latest book, *He Calls Me Friend*, challenges us to enter into deep friendship
not only with others around us but, most importantly, with the triune God of the
Scriptures. In a world that is as divided as ours, we need deep, lasting, and "gracist"
friendships. This book helps us get there!

**DAVID ANDERSON**
Executive Director of Lydia Home Association and Founder of Safe Families for
Children

As a friend of God the Father, John Perkins lets God lead him. As a friend of God, the
Son, John Perkins is a foot-washer who is a humble servant of God. As a friend of God
the Spirit, John Perkins exemplifies friend-raising rather than fund-raising. As a friend
to all of us, John Perkins has written a wonderful book, *He Calls Me Friend*.

**PATRICK McCASKEY**
Chicago Bears Vice President and Chairman of Sports Faith International

John Perkins is my friend, a living legend that every leader should study and seek to imitate because he loves well. I come from a generation that likes to talk about issues of gospel justice and reconciliation. John has lived it, without compromise, for decades. I believe *He Calls Me Friend* is one of the most important books of our day, from one of the last living prophets of the civil rights era. If we are to see the change we desperately need, understanding friendship (God's way) might just be the key.

**NICK HALL**
Founder of Pulse movement, author of *Reset: Jesus Changes Everything*

Dr. Perkins has now issued a book, *He Calls Me Friend*, not only about the importance of human friendship in his life, but about the "friendship" aspect of our relationship with God. Jesus claims the apostles as "friends" in John 15:13–15. "You are my friends if you do what I command" indicates that a great imbalance of authority need not be a barrier to friendship! And much earlier, Abraham was known as the "friend of God." C. S. Lewis said that in his time, "friendship" was looked down upon compared to Affection and Eros. I hope that this book will help to restore the status of Friendship to where it belongs.

**HOWARD AHMANSON**
Philanthropist

Not many men move me to tears, but Dr. John Perkins does. This gospel hero was a friend to my dad years ago, and now he is a friend to me, which moves me. When Dr. Perkins writes about friendship, he means it. I believe his new book, *He Calls Me Friend*, will move you too, especially in these days of anger and division. We need the friendship message of this book, and we need it *now*.

**RAY ORTLUND**
Immanuel Church, Nashville

Wow! It's time John Perkins wrote this book about friendship. He is the consummate endearment of a friend. John Perkins is a great friend of thousands! *He Calls Me Friend* is his written description of friendship. This friendship begins with God and then pours into the lives of other people. I love this book! What a privilege it is to have John Perkins call me a friend. You will be inspired and equipped to be friends with God and other people by this book. I without hesitation highly recommended this book to all.

**WAYNE GORDON**
Founder of Lawndale Community Church and Chairman of Christian Community Development Association

# HE
# CALLS
# ME
# *friend*

## The Healing Power
## of Friendship in a Lonely World

JOHN M. PERKINS
with KAREN WADDLES

**MOODY PUBLISHERS**

CHICAGO

Edited by: Pamela J. Pugh
Interior design: Ragont Design
Randy & Joan Nabors photo: Rachel Douglass Photography
Author photo: Will Sterling, Sterling Photography
Cover design: Erik M. Peterson
Cover photo of two friends copyright © 2019 by BONNINSTUDIO / Stocksy (2489258). All rights reserved.

Library of Congress Cataloging-in-Publication Data

Names: Perkins, John, 1930- author. | Waddles, Karen, author.
Title: He calls me friend : the healing power of friendship in a lonely world
 / John Perkins with Karen Waddles.
Description: Chicago : Moody Publishers, [2019] | Includes bibliographical
 references. |
Identifiers: LCCN 2019017450 (print) | LCCN 2019020754 (ebook) | ISBN
 9780802497963 () | ISBN 9780802419361
Subjects: LCSH: Friendship--Religious aspects--Christianity.
Classification: LCC BV4647.F7 (ebook) | LCC BV4647.F7 P47 2019 (print) |
DDC
 241/.6762--dc23
LC record available at https://lccn.loc.gov/2019017450

ISBN: 978-0-8024-1936-1

We hope you enjoy this book from Moody Publishers. Our goal is to provide high-quality, thought-provoking books and products that connect truth to your real needs and challenges. For more information on other books and products written and produced from a biblical perspective, go to www.moodypublishers. com or write to:

Moody Publishers
820 North La Salle Boulevard
Chicago, IL 60610

1 3 5 7 9 10 8 6 4 2

*Printed in the United States of America*

To my Eternal Friend and to every friend who has walked with me since I entered the kingdom more than sixty-two years ago. To those who He used to undergird me in my pain, to give me hope when I had none, and to encourage me to keep moving forward . . . there would not be enough time or space to name every one of you and, because our friendship is so precious, I dare not risk missing or offending anyone. To each and every one of you . . . thank you for being with me through my life's journey . . . thank you for being a friend.

# Contents

Foreword   9

Introduction   13

## PART ONE: FRIENDSHIP WITH GOD THE FATHER

1. The Hound of Heaven Who Pursues   27

2. The Intimate, Holy One   41

3. The Great Forgiver   55

    Let's Hear It from Ken Smith: "Friendship Is Forever"   66

## PART TWO: FRIENDSHIP WITH JESUS

4. The God Who Came to Us   73

5. Friend of Prostitutes, Thieves, and the Outsider   85

    Let's Hear It from Randy and Joan Nabors:
    "Friendship Is Tolerant"   95

## PART THREE: FRIENDSHIP WITH THE HOLY SPIRIT

6. The God Who Dwells Within   101

7. The Fruit of Friendship   113

    Let's Hear It from Wayne Gordon: "Friendship
    Means Going Deep"   127

## PART FOUR: FRIENDSHIP WITH OTHERS

8. Crossing Hard Lines     133
9. The Friendship Challenge     145

Let's Hear It from Phillip Perkins: "My Daddy,
My Friend"     155

Conclusion     159
To Think About and Talk Over     165
Notes     171
Acknowledgments     175

# Foreword

'll never forget the first time I met Dr. John Perkins. He just radiates the love of Jesus and has a smile that lights up the room. If you've met him, you know what I mean. He's magnetic. We invited him to speak to our community a few years ago—for his help, counsel, wisdom, and because of his life's work against the ravaging effects of racism. We wanted to be more intentional than ever to address the issues of racial reconciliation in this country and how we could be part of the solution. I had no idea what I was in for. I sat down for a conversation with Dr. Perkins and I, along with our community, were sitting on the edge of our seats. None of us who were there that day will ever be the same. He and I became fast friends and as they say, the rest is history.

Now I know the job of any good interviewer is to do his homework but I humbly confess I had only time to briefly skim his most recent book. In the rush to make schedules work and to get him there, I didn't have many of the details of his story, so by the time he sat down with me for our conversation, I wasn't prepared in more ways than one. The more he talked, the more futile my questions felt because all I wanted was to listen and then listen some more. I felt all these things that day: outrage, disbelief, compassion, and overwhelming love for Dr. Perkins. He shared his life with us in stories—stories of his mother dying due to extreme poverty, how his brother was brutally murdered by a white police officer, how God turned his anger into action and what is now an unmatched life and legacy of amazing faith. It was unbelievable how he openly shared with so much strength and humility and grace. He generously shared his life with us, complete strangers. Even through tears, his presence filled me with so much hope. I was left undone but invigorated.

Dr. Perkins has penned this work, *He Calls Me Friend,* with such beauty and authenticity because he's kept it pretty simple. He has chosen to know God and make Him known. He has chosen to receive the friendship of God, much like a modern-day apostle John, the self- proclaimed disciple Jesus loved so much. More precisely, he has chosen to fully embrace God the Father, His Son Jesus, and the Holy Spirit. And Dr. Perkins's life has testified to the reality of this friendship time after time, challenge after challenge, and season after season. Just like Jesus' life, I see so clearly what makes Dr. Perkins's life and message so compelling. Jesus' life was filled with people—men and women He encountered and then embraced. Everyday people He ate meals with, weddings He attended, children He embraced, women He protected, and even a friend He brought back from the dead. Friends whose sorrows He shared and ultimately whose sin He assumed. He left for us a beautiful picture of godly friendship that was heart to heart and broke all the rules.

And just like that, I am provoked all over again by John Perkins sharing his life with me. Just as I was when we first met. I've often thought about him over the years and am still awestruck at how he's endured what he has endured—and he's smiling. I've even had very loud (well, okay I may have been shouting) conversations with God about it, asking, "Lord, how?!"

"How has this man endured such pain, cruelty, and injustice and still be so SWEET?!"

Listen, it's one thing to be sweet when someone takes your parking space, but what my friend has endured is unspeakable, yet he loves on. Only a man who has experienced an incredibly intimate level of friendship with God is able to help me believe that all things are possible like this. He makes me want to know God more. He inspires me to be a constant companion of God. Only a man who knows Jesus intimately and has cultivated a real and thriving relationship with Him can give us this kind of hope that we really can win the fight against the sin of racism.

Yes, Dr. Perkins and I we were once strangers but we are strangers no more. We are friends who have become family. I knew that day that my relationship with Dr. Perkins was one I wanted for a lifetime. He embraced me, my family and the Churchome community—complete strangers—and calls us friends. We have formed a friendship I am forever changed by. He is a national treasure, a representation of hope and change we all need. We enjoy a true friendship that is marked by safety and sacrifice, of being committed to one another with the conviction that only God can give. Not the loosely defined friendship that culture promotes but a friendship that is cultivated in sincere love and respect for one another. A friendship that shares burdens and endures sorrows. This kind of friendship is the only kind, bound by the love of God and for one another, that can overcome and win this fight against hate and bigotry. Jesus does indeed call him friend, and I'm so very grateful I get to as well.

JUDAH SMITH
Lead Pastor of Churchome and *NY Times*
bestselling author of *Jesus Is _____.*

"*I have called you friends.*"

John 15:15

# Introduction

New Zealand has long been known for its tranquility, good quality of life, and economic freedom. My wife and I visited there some time ago and were struck by the beauty and the peacefulness of that nation. Vera Mae said that if she could live anywhere other than the United States, she'd choose to live there.

As I pen the words to this book, our hearts are breaking with the news that a gunman murdered fifty Muslims at their places of worship in the city of Christchurch. This country, which for many years has been peaceful and safe, is now scarred by ethnic hatred and violence. This sad scene follows closely behind the killing of eleven Jews at the Tree of Life Synagogue in Pittsburgh, Pennsylvania, and the murder of a young white woman in Charlottesville, Virginia, who protested the chants of white supremacists as they marched through the streets displaying Nazi symbols.

I've lived long enough to not be alarmed by much of anything, but I see something happening in our country and across the world right now that we've got to get ahold of. If we don't, it will destroy us.

When I wrote *One Blood: Parting Words to the Church on Race and Love*, it was in my heart to press upon people to know that there is only one race—the human race. And that every human being is created in the image of God and has dignity and worth. Each individual—black, white, Hispanic, Asian, Jewish, Muslim—is created in God's image! With all my heart I believe that the church is responsible for knowing that truth and modeling it in how we live. *One Blood* was a paradigm shift.

13

Our behavior showed that we thought there were many races: a black race, a white race, a Hispanic race, an Asian race, and so on. But in truth there is only one, and we are identical to one another with the exception of 0.1 percent of our makeup that accounts for our skin color and physical appearance.

This book is the progression of that message. It's the discipleship message that follows after we are saved by the blood of Jesus. How do we live out this new paradigm of oneness? How do we move beyond the boundaries and the walls that have separated us along ethnic, economic, social, and class lines? Is there a healing balm for the sin sickness of ethnic hatred and prejudice?

The apostle John said it most clearly in Scripture: "If we walk in the light, as he is in the light, we have fellowship [friendship] with one another" (1 John 1:7a). My argument is that friendship is the way across and through the lines that have separated us for so long. Friendship is discipleship in action. God calls us into a deep friendship with Himself and with all His children that is in sharp contrast to how we talk about "friends" today. There's been a lot of talk about friendship because of Facebook and the internet. You can collect friends and "likes" and begin to feel pretty good about yourself, depending on

> We may be "connected," but we're lonely, we're isolated from each other, and we've become afraid of each other.

how many you accumulate. Our foundation, the John & Vera Mae Perkins Foundation, has about 3,500 likes right now, and I suppose that's pretty good. But I'm not sure that's the kind of friendship that is strong enough to carry us through and across the hard lines that have isolated us from each other. I think you can actually have a lot of those kinds of friends and still be lonely, separated, and afraid.

Columnist E. J. Dionne Jr. tells of a conversation Marc Dunkelman had twenty years ago with his grandfather, a retired salesman. They talked about how to find the best restaurants in an unfamiliar city. Marc was excited about a new app that would make it easy for people to find the best places to eat and that would even show them which restaurants were nearby. But his grandfather was not as eager to embrace this new technology. He said that whenever he went on a sales trip to a new place he would look for a "friendly looking stranger" and ask him to recommend a good place to eat. In the process this stranger would often become a new friend and someone that he would see when he returned to the city. "That's how I got to understand the world—by talking to strangers," the older man said. "With all these fancy technologies you're talking about, how are people going to get to know one another? You ask me, I think it's going to make everyone lonely."[1]

I think he's right. We have all the technology that should make it easier for us to reach out to one another, but we're not really touching one another. We may be "connected," but we're lonely, we're isolated from each other, and we've become afraid of each other. That fear has produced acts of violence that are becoming all too common.

Loneliness has been called "one of the greatest public health challenges of our time."[2] The prime minister of England has even appointed a minister of loneliness to address the problem.[3] In the United States, the American Association of Retired Persons (AARP) did research on adults who are forty-five years and older. They discovered that one-third of them are lonely.[4] There's an epidemic of loneliness and friendlessness. And this epidemic has serious public health consequences. Research has shown that loneliness and isolation are just as bad for our health as smoking fifteen cigarettes a day and can speed up the advance of Alzheimer's disease.[5]

So friendlessness, loneliness, and isolation do damage to our bodies, to our minds—and to our souls. And it's the impact on our souls that this book addresses. I want to talk about friendship at the soul level. I think that's the kind of friendship that God intended for us to have: with Him and with others. That's the only kind of friendship that will heal our soul wound and help us fix this ethnic problem. I like these two definitions of friendship. The first comes from a theological wordbook, and the second comes from the Native American culture:

> "Friendship is a reciprocal relationship
> characterized by intimacy, faithfulness,
> trust, unmotivated kindness,
> and service."[6]
> Friend: "One-who-carries-my-
> sorrows-on-his-back."[7]

That's what friendship is. It's being able to hook up with someone and walk through life together. It's trusting in and caring for one another at a deep heart level. It's helping one another carry the sorrows of life.

My very first friend was my grandmother. She was old, but she really was my first friend. When I felt downcast or when somebody did something to me and I couldn't get back at them, I'd cry and go sit by the fireplace. And I'd put my head in her lap. Her fragile hands would stroke my troubled head and some of my sadness would go away. She became a safe place for me . . . like an anchor in stormy waters.

That was important for me as a child growing up poor in Mississippi in the Jim Crow South. My mother died when I was seven months old. She took me to her breast and gave me her last ounce of strength. She died of starvation and, because it would have been difficult for my father to raise us alone, I was left to be mothered by my grandmother, who raised thirteen children. She did the best she could and I'm grateful that she took me in. Our house was always filled with children but I still felt alone.

Maybe I was especially needy because my mother was gone and my father was absent from the home. I always struggled to see how or if my life mattered. Early on I wanted to know that I was important, that my life carried some kind of significance. I felt unimportant and very alone.

If it's true that our significance is reflected in the eyes of others, then I suppose I was at a great deficit as a poor black boy in Mississippi. There were no doting parents who looked with pride at my first steps or who listened with anticipation for my first words. There were no teachers whose eyes lit up when I walked into the classroom. But I am forever grateful for one teacher. Mrs. Maybelle Armstrong taught me the stories of Nat Turner, Frederick Douglass, and John Brown, and encouraged me that I too could one day be a leader. This gave me a deep love for my blackness and it kept me from feeling like I was less human than anyone else. Maybe she could see something in me—even as a young boy—that I could not see in myself. But somewhere between third and fifth grade, I stopped going to school and went to work picking cotton.

I learned more lessons about my insignificance in the cotton fields of Mississippi. On one particular day the lesson was so raw and cut so deep that I still remember it more than

HE CALLS ME FRIEND

seventy years later, just like it was yesterday. When I was eleven or twelve, I worked a whole day hauling hay for a white gentleman. I was expecting to get a dollar or a dollar and a half for that day of work. But at the end of the day he gave me a dime and a buffalo nickel. Even as a child I understood that by his actions he was saying that I had no value or worth.

> **I guess we had almost achieved the American dream . . . but something was still missing. I was unsettled, but I didn't know why.**

A few years later when my brother Clyde was killed by a police officer, I learned that a black man's life wasn't worth much of anything, at least not in Mississippi. So, like Christian in *Pilgrim's Progress*, I set out to find the Celestial City, a place where my life mattered, and where the huge void of insignificance could be filled. My pilgrimage took me to California. It truly was like the Celestial City to a black man from the South. I was able to find a good job there. I saw my worth and value reflected in the eyes of people I met, both black and white.

My best fortune was marrying Vera Mae and beginning to build a family together. Finally, life was good. I guess we had almost achieved the American dream. I had true friends, a family, a nice house, a good job, and people who respected me . . . but something was still missing. I was unsettled, but I didn't know why. There was a deep, deep longing—a loneliness—in my heart that would not go away.

Our oldest son, Spencer, began going to Good News Club meetings, where he learned that the Bible taught that Jesus loves him. He would come home eager to share the stories he

had learned with me. When he invited me to go, I was more excited than he could have ever known. And when I began reading
the Bible for myself, from the very first pages I found the answer
to that deep, deep longing, the loneliness that felt like a wide,
empty chasm. I read about a God who would be a friend. For
the very first time I read about a God who created everything:
the earth, the sun, moon, stars, and every living creature. Then
He created a man and a woman. Poet James Weldon Johnson
imagines the scene. In "The Creation," Johnson depicts God ob-
serving the grandeur of all that He had made. After a time, the
Lord decided it wasn't enough, that something was missing. He
decided, "I'll make me a man."[8]

So He did.

I love that picture of God, sitting and thinking about what
He would do to fill His "loneliness," to create a being that He
could fellowship with, and finally deciding that He would make
a man. It might not be theologically accurate, since God—
Father, Son, and Holy Spirit—actually was complete in Himself. And to tell the truth, I'm pretty sure we were birthed out
of the friendship of the Trinity. When God said in Genesis 1:26,
"Let us make mankind in our image, in our likeness," He set
things in motion.

But in my mind's eye I can imagine God bending down and
scooping up clay, smoothing out the rough places and carefully forming the body of Adam, the first human being. Like
a sculptor, He stands back from His masterpiece, taking in
the beauty of what He has made. Surely this must have been
the image that the psalmist had in mind when he wrote that
we are "fearfully and wonderfully made" (Ps. 139:14). And finally God kissed life into Adam. "And the man became a living
being" (Gen. 2:7).

Amazingly, after God put the first man, Adam, in the garden of Eden, where he had everything he could possibly need, God said, "It is not good for the man to be alone. I will make a helper suitable for him" (Gen. 2:18). So God created a woman with the rib from Adam's side and named her Eve. Her beauty thrilled Adam and he found in her an answer to his loneliness. Friendship and relationship are the remedies for loneliness and isolation. And theirs was a rich, intimate friendship. Adam "knew" Eve. This word carries the idea of physical and emotional intimacy. God had provided a solution for the loneliness that threatened to occupy the garden. God intended for marriage to be like that: for husband and wife to fill each other's lonely place.

You can watch a couple walking in the park and can almost tell if they are married or not. Something about their behavior . . . how they hold hands, how they walk in step with each other. There's an unspoken union that is evident because they are one. When Vera Mae and I got married, I was enthralled with her beauty. To think that she was now a part of me! I would never be alone again. And for these past sixty-nine years, this has been one of my greatest treasures. We have been one.

There was a unique friendship and love between Adam and Eve, and also with God. I believe that God visited them every day in the garden because they were friends. Dr. Bill Thrasher suggests that God "made man with a special care and design, apart from everything else, to be able to enjoy Him in all His perfection. To talk, to walk, to think, to play together. It may be hard for you to imagine going for a walk in the park with God, but that's exactly what Adam and Eve enjoyed."[9] Just the thought of being able to have that kind of relationship with God excited me. I could almost feel the hole in my heart beginning to fill up—could I ever be friends with *this* God?

The tranquil friendship in the garden was cut short because Adam and Eve broke the rules. And broke the heart of God. The one tree that God told them not to eat of—the tree of the knowledge of good and evil—was too tempting. They disobeyed God; and suddenly shame entered that place of intimacy, love, and friendship. He removed them from the garden, and it could have all ended there. But God made it clear—even before

> Friendship is the ship we are meant to take along our pilgrim journey, loving one another, and even laying down our lives for one another if necessary.

they left the garden for the last time—that He was not going to give up on intimate friendship and loving relationship with mankind. He promised that He would restore the friendship forever through one who would come through the lineage of Adam and Eve (see Gen. 3:15). The New Testament book of Luke shows that God did exactly what He said He would do. Luke traces the lineage of Jesus all the way back to Adam (Luke 3:23–38).

So I kept reading and reading and at the end of it all there's talk about a new heaven and a new earth. And there's a picture of this same God enjoying eternal friendship and relationship with everyone who chooses to be His friend. What begins to emerge for me is the crucial importance of friendship and relationship with this awesome God. This is friendship at the soul level! Without it, we are left with a gaping wound in our souls. It's a hole that loneliness and anger fill up and seep out of.

In my eighty-nine years on this earth, I have come to believe that the purpose of man is to know this awesome God—to love Him, serve Him, and worship Him—and to make Him known. And I believe that God has not only made us for that and commanded us to do that, but in His grace He has also shown us how. He has shown us the way. And it is through friendship. This "having fellowship with one another," that He makes possible, is the revolution that can heal the centuries' old hurts and hatreds that divide us. Because we are friends with Him, we do not have to cross these divides alone. We are not meant to. Friendship is the ship we are meant to take along our pilgrim journey, loving one another, and even laying down our lives for one another if necessary.[10]

I believe that God models perfectly for us what this kind of biblical friendship looks like. It pursues, even those who are unlikely, unqualified, and unworthy. Biblical friendship goes deep. It doesn't settle for surface talk. Biblical friendship forgives and does so without limit. We'll talk about Abraham, Moses, and David as friends of God in Part One: Friendship with God the Father. We'll examine powerful lessons about friendship in how God related to each of these people, and how they responded.

Biblical friendship reaches across lines of ethnicity, gender, and social status. Jesus showed us how to do that, and in Part Two: Friendship with Jesus, we'll talk about that. He was God in the flesh, yet He came as a helpless child born to a virgin. He came in humility—not at all what you would expect of a king. He was a friend of prostitutes, tax collectors, and lepers. He showed us how to reach across and show love to people who don't look like us. He modeled true friendship when He gave His life for His friends.

Part Three will introduce us to the concept of being friends with the Holy Spirit. I think there's a lot of confusion about who He is. He's not a mist that floats through the air. He is the God who lives within the heart of every believer. His work in helping us live out the friendship mandate is crucial. From the very moment that He came at Pentecost He came to help people become friends of God. He rushed on the scene at Pentecost and translated the gospel into every language spoken by the crowds present that day so that everyone could hear and understand the message from God. The message was that Jesus had come as the God-man and had died for their sins, so that finally the friendship that had been broken in the garden of Eden could be restored forever. And the Holy Spirit is the one who knits our hearts together in fellowship and friendship. He makes us one.

And finally, in Part Four: Friendship with Others, we will talk about how being a friend of God calls us to extend that friendship and love to others. We'll learn from the Good Samaritan, Esther and Mordecai, and others. We'll be challenged to cross the hard lines that have separated us for much too long. If ever there was a time that this message is needed, the time is now. The growing epidemic of loneliness, isolation, and anger in our world is a platform for the friendship that God offers to everyone who will receive it.

Along the way I'll share some special friend stories. My life has been enriched by a multitude of friends. There would not be enough pages in this book to talk about all of them. The persons who have been chosen to share their stories in this book are symbolic and representative of the overflowing bounty of friends who, like my grandmother and like the great God of creation, have been safe harbors for me. I've invited them to share their stories of how God brought us together, and how those friendships have enriched our lives.

The book will conclude with a personal challenge to become a friend of God and a friend to others. This is the only thing that will follow us from this life into the next: friends we have helped to find the way to the one true Friend. Israel Houghton sings, "I am a friend of God . . . He calls me friend." I love the words to this song. I encourage you to meditate on these words as we move forward. Let your mind be blown by the truth that the Great God of Glory calls you friend, and He wants the abundance of love that He gives to you to overflow in love for others.

*Part One*

---

# FRIENDSHIP WITH GOD THE FATHER

"But you, Israel, my servant, Jacob, whom I have chosen, you descendants of Abraham my friend, I took you from the ends of the earth, from its farthest corners I called you. I said 'You are my servant'; I have chosen you and have not rejected you."

Isaiah 41:8–9

"Our God, did you not drive out the inhabitants of this land before your people Israel and give it forever to the descendants of Abraham your friend?"

2 Chronicles 20:7

# CHAPTER 1

# The Hound of Heaven Who Pursues

*Marty Nesbitt was known as the "first friend." When Barack Obama ran for the presidency in 2008 he instituted a "no more new friends" rule. He decided to surround himself with trusted, longtime friends who could help keep him grounded. He shared something special with Marty. They both had had disappointing relationships with their fathers and decided that they would be great dads to their own children. They shared a deep father wound that was a bond and a motivator for both men.[1]*

Abraham was "first friend" with God. We infer from God's interaction with Adam and Eve in the garden that they were friends, but Abraham was the first man God referred to in the Bible as His friend. I love the story of Abraham. When I first read through the Bible I understood why God would call him "friend." I think that when people share common experiences it creates a bond that true relationship can be built on.

Traumatic experiences have a way of creating bonds that are unique and lasting.

Some of the bonds I shared with others who fought for civil rights went so deep because we risked our lives just to register people to vote. This didn't sit well with some of the local whites in Mendenhall, Mississippi. We started getting threatening phone calls, and cars started showing up at night, driving real slowly past our house. When I shared all this with some of my neighbors, the community jumped into action. Almost a hundred men arrived each night to protect my house. They told me to go to bed and get some rest. "We'll protect you and your family," they said to me. "You are here to do what we can't do, and it's our task to protect you."[2] This common experience served as a foundation that led to lasting friendships between us. I would never forget their personal sacrifice for me.

God's request of Abraham created a common bond between Him and Abraham that was unique. He asked Abraham to do something that He never asked another human being to do. It was the ultimate sacrifice. And Abraham obeyed. That common experience, I believe, established Abraham forever as a friend of God like no one else. Keep reading!

## THE GOD WHO SEEKS

Abraham grew up in the city of Ur, which was known for its worship of many gods. We know from Joshua 24:2 that Abraham and his father, Terah, worshiped idols. They would bring their offerings to the temples for their gods in hope that they would provide protection and would favor them. The people of Ur believed that the moon god, Nanna, was the greatest god because he provided fertility for their crops, herds, and families.

For seventy-five years Abraham had believed that he needed

to give things to these gods in order to be safe, in order to prosper. And suddenly God came to Abraham, seeking after him, and promising to bless him. I love that! I couldn't believe that this God, who was the God of creation, would lower himself to seek out Abraham as a friend and promise to bless him! This is not an ordinary god. This is the God who seeks relationship. This is a God who reaches out, who seeks friends to love and bless.

> **God loves you, and He wants you. How does this truth challenge what you've previously believed about Him?**

I learned early on that if you want a friend, you have to be a friend. That's what God did. He didn't wait for Abraham to look for Him or to give him things. He pursued Abraham. He's like that. Francis Thompson wrote a poem titled "The Hound of Heaven," that pictures God as one who tirelessly pursues and follows after His prey like a hound chasing a rabbit. He follows after, never turning away, until the soul feels the weight of His pursuit and turns to Him. This idea that God is relentlessly pursuing us is beyond comprehension. The Song of Solomon uses the picture of a bridegroom pursuing his beloved to represent God's passionate love and desire for us to be friends and experience His purpose for our lives. This pursuit lasts for a lifetime. It first calls us into His embrace as friend and then repeatedly draws us toward His plan for our lives.

I don't know how you see God. Some people see Him as a doting grandfather who is quietly watching over us. Other people see Him as an angry drill sergeant who is never pleased with us and always demanding more than we can give.

Abraham's story reminds me that God is so full of love that He seeks us out wherever we are and lavishes us with His love. Here's how God talked about His love for us: "Can a mother forget the baby at her breast and have no compassion on the child she has borne? Though she may forget, I will not forget you! See, I have engraved you on the palms of my hands; your walls are ever before me" (Isa. 49:15–16). Think about that for a moment. God loves you, and He wants you. How does this truth challenge what you've previously believed about Him?

## THE GOD WHO PROMISES

God told Abraham, then called Abram, to leave his kinfolk and everything that he was familiar with and just go. With the promise that God would show him where he was to go, Abraham was told to leave his homeland and trust that God would make him into a great nation, and that everybody on earth would be blessed through him. So, at seventy-five years of age, Abraham set out on his pilgrimage. "So Abram went, as the LORD had told him" (Gen. 12:4).

Twenty-five years later, God reminded Abraham of this promise and He entered into a covenant with him (see Gen. 15). In that covenant He told Abraham that his descendants would be slaves for four hundred years and would be set free to live in the land that He would give them. In order for that to happen, God would have to miraculously give Abraham a son. By this time Abraham was one hundred years old and his wife, Sarah, was ninety. This was no small miracle. It was so impossible to imagine that both Abraham and Sarah laughed when they heard the announcement (Gen. 17:17; 18:12). But they were both getting ready to learn that this God not only reaches out to seek relationship, He keeps His promises.

I am blown away by the fact that God would make promises to any man. But He did that again and again. He obligated Himself to men.

> So do not fear, for I am with you; do not be dismayed, for I am your God. I will strengthen you and help you; I will uphold you with my righteous right hand. —Isaiah 41:10

> When you pass through the waters, I will be with you; and when you pass through the rivers, they will not sweep over you. When you walk through the fire, you will not be burned; the flames will not set you ablaze. —Isaiah 43:2

> "For I know the plans I have for you," declares the LORD, "plans to prosper you and not to harm you, plans to give you hope and a future." —Jeremiah 29:11

God makes promises, and His promises are sure. The ultimate promise is the promise of eternal life for those who believe that Jesus Christ is the Son of God. If you are a friend of God, He can get you there. The whole Bible was written to help us know the promise of God, and to restore us to what He intended for us. We can rest in the truth of the words of that old hymn:[3]

> Standing on the promises that cannot fail,
> When the howling storms of doubt and fear assail,
> By the living Word of God I shall prevail,
> Standing on the promises of God.

Everything God says He will do . . . He does. Though they waited many years after His promise to Abraham and Sarah, their son, Isaac, was born. As someone who is more than eighty years old, I take heart from the fact that God waited until Abraham was an old man before He used him. He could have called Abraham out of Ur when he was a young man, strong and full of energy. But He waited until Abraham was diminished and up in age. I like that. It proves that God is not a respecter of persons. Our world has a way of putting old folks on the shelf and ignoring the wisdom of the ages. But God is not like that. He desires friendship with everyone, even those who are well past their productive years according to the world's standards.

When John Glenn boarded the space shuttle on October 29, 1998, at the age of seventy-seven, *Time* magazine ran an article that began by saying, "This is no country for old men." The opinion of most folks is that at the age of seventy-seven, a man should be sitting in a rocking chair at a retirement home, collecting Social Security. He should move aside so the young folks can take over. I'm grateful that God still calls old people today—and He has abundant purpose for each of those lives until the very end. I'm finding that even at the age of eighty-nine He has still got things for me to do in this life. Actually the complete quote from *Time* goes on and gets it right: "This is no country for old men, so John Glenn will be leaving it in October—will quit the entire planet and head out for a realm where age doesn't count."[4] God certainly works through us in a realm where age doesn't matter!

## GOD DEMANDS TRUST

Again and again, I read that Abraham believed God. Abraham believed God. But I think the thing that really cemented Abraham's friendship with God was what happened when God told him to sacrifice his son Isaac. "Then God said, 'Take your son, your only son, whom you love—Isaac—and go to the region of

Moriah. Sacrifice him there as a burnt offering on a mountain I will show you'" (Gen. 22:2). Early the next morning, Abraham got up. He loaded up his donkey, cut the wood for the burnt offering, took Isaac and two of his servants along as he headed out in obedience to God. Abraham would have been familiar with the horrific practice of child sacrifice because it was common in the city of Ur. But Isaac was not an infant or young child. He was most likely a teen or young adult,[5] and his heart was knit together with his father's heart. And Abraham had left the pagan practices of his upbringing and was following God faithfully. But he followed God's command in faith.

I can identify with the grief and struggle that Abraham faced. The thought of losing a child is unspeakable. It shakes your foundation. When our son Spencer died, I almost lost my will to live. I had envisioned passing on my life's work to him; and he was gone. And years later when our youngest son, Wayne, died, I visited the land of mourning once again. The pain was hard to put into words.

But God commanded Abraham to give up Isaac, his only son, to test whether he really trusted him or not. And Abraham met the test. Just as he was preparing to take Isaac's life, God stopped him and pointed out a ram in the bush. When Abraham sacrificed the ram, he declared that the place would be known as "The LORD Will Provide." I think this was the turning point in Abraham's friendship with God. God would never ask another father to sacrifice his son on an altar . . . until He Himself would do that in offering Jesus as a sacrifice for the sins of the world. I think Abraham learned that friendship with God is all or nothing. God expects that kind of all-or-nothing surrender because He gives us His all. In the words of A. W. Tozer: "An infinite God can give all of Himself to each of His children. He does not distribute Himself that each may have a part, but to each one He gives all of Himself as fully as if there were no others."[6]

## ABRAHAM FOUND THE PEARL

I've often asked the question, what did Abraham give up and what did he gain when he chose to be a friend of God? He gave up everything. He walked away from his homeland, his birthplace, the customs he had been raised with. He walked away from considerable wealth. I believe that Abraham discovered that friendship with God was like the pearl of great price. Matthew 13:45–46 tells us what Jesus said: "The kingdom of heaven is like a merchant looking for fine pearls. When he found one of great value, he went away and sold everything he had and bought it."

Abraham discovered the true pearl. He found out that the only way to this awesome, all-knowing God was by faith. He gave up everything and began a pilgrimage of faith, trusting God every day for direction. And along the way he learned about God's faithfulness. Friendship with God means leaving everything else behind . . . especially our prejudices and wrong notions about people who don't look like us.

## ANSWERING GOD'S CALL TO FRIENDSHIP

When God calls you to something, He calls you first to Himself as friend, then He calls you to work for Him. When the vision is big enough, it's worth giving up everything you have to follow that vision. When I think of someone who gave up everything, I think of Jim Elliot. He was a missionary to Ecuador. He knew that the Huaorani people (formerly known as the Aucas) were violent and had had no contact with the outside world. He understood the risk he was taking when he and four other missionaries landed their plane and waited to be approached by the people. At first the people seemed to receive them well, but they soon became suspicious and afraid that they were being taken advantage of. "They decided they should kill the visitors before they were themselves killed."[7] They speared Jim and his friends to death and left their bodies in the water. Jim Elliot believed that being a friend of God was worth giving up everything, even your life, so that people who didn't look like him could become friends of God.

After Jim's death, his wife, Elisabeth, got to know two of the women from the tribe. She, along with Rachel Saint, the sister of Nate, another of the murdered missionaries, was invited to come back and tell them about God. She lived with the Huaorani for two years and many of them became friends of God, and Rachel remained with them for thirty years. I became acquainted with Elisabeth when she would come to Mississippi to visit her daughter and son-in-law. Our paths often crossed at the airport as we were both heading out to answer God's call on our lives. I admired the bravery both she and Jim had in taking God's message to such a dangerous place. Jim gave up everything in response to God's call on his life. And it provided an open door for many people to know the God he called friend.

I learned something about the call of God when we were in Monrovia, California. In some ways my background was like Abraham's. I didn't grow up worshiping God in Mississippi. My people were not Christians. We didn't go to church. We were known for being outlaws and for our bootlegging business. It was a badge of honor that we could outwit the man by making money on the side to survive. The system of sharecropping was rigged against us from the beginning, so we became experts at finding other ways to make money. A lot of those ways had us at odds with the law, so good church people looked down their noses at us. My concept of God was tainted by my view of church folk; I didn't have a good feeling about either one.

But when I went to California and became a part of a church and got to really know God, things changed. I was discipled by a white woman who had served as a missionary to Brazil for nineteen years. Many missionaries came home after World War II and realized that our own country was a huge mission field. Americans need the gospel as much as people in developing countries do. After I was converted, I told her that I wanted to be a Bible teacher. She helped me see that the Bible was the revelation of God and that if I was going to be a Bible teacher I needed to know the whole story. When I got to chapter 12 of Genesis, I felt my call from God, very much like His call to Abraham.

> Like Abraham, I learned that God is always seeking, always drawing. He draws us first into relationship with Him as friend. And then He continually draws us into more intimate fellowship with Him and toward the plan He has for our life.

But our life was comfortable. We finally had everything we dreamed of . . . a nice twelve-room house, a well-paying job as a welder, a growing family, and a loving church. I began doing evangelistic work at a prison work camp that had been set up in the San Gabriel Valley by the California Youth Authority. The camp was filled with black teenage boys. Most of them had come from the South. I was sure that if they had heard about

Jesus and His love for them earlier in their childhoods, like our son Spencer, they would have had a better chance at life.

When I shared my story with them, two of them who were sitting in the back were crying. When I looked at them, I realized that I was looking at myself. That could have been me sitting behind prison walls wasting away. I don't know what ultimately happened to those two boys in that prison, but I know that my life has not been the same since that day. I had sworn that I would never return to Mississippi to live. I had nothing but bad memories when I thought about Mississippi. But I felt God calling our family to give up everything and go back to serve Him there. In a lesser way than Abraham heard it, I felt like God was asking me to give up my comfortable life and to trust Him to make me a blessing to others. Maybe I could help young boys in Mississippi; I could tell them that God wanted to be their friend and keep them from ending up in prison.

Like Abraham, I learned that God is always seeking, always drawing. He draws us first into relationship with Him as friend. And then He continually draws us into more intimate fellowship with Him and toward the plan He has for our life. He was drawing me back to Mississippi when I was in California. He has a way of drawing you that lets you know it could only be Him. Because of the weight of everything we had left behind in Mississippi—the anger, the bitterness, the bad memories—it would take nothing less than a God-sized purpose to convince us to return to the South to live and serve.

## GOING BACK? NO— GOING FORWARD WITH GOD

We did move back to Mississippi. And I learned that God keeps His promises. He promised me that if I obeyed Him and went back to Mississippi, He would take care of our family. And He did that. He allowed us to share the gospel with the destitute, alcoholics, and unchurched teenagers walking the streets and wasting themselves in the honky-tonks in New Hebron, Mississippi.[8] He brought us through being jailed and beaten, and having our lives threatened.

He gave us a testimony for Him. He showed us that He has the power to bridge the divide between people who don't look like each other. Where hatred had been sown, He showed us that love and friendship can uproot those ugly seeds. I think about that a lot when I reflect on what's happening in our country today. We are divided as we have never been before. We've allowed the color of our skin and other differences to separate us and keep us from being friends. I believe that God is calling all of us to His great vision of reconciliation—biblical friendship. That's a calling that's bigger than any one of us; but not big at all if we work together with His power.

We learned that being a friend of God is worth giving up everything else for. Possessions. Popularity. Prejudices. Power. Friendship with God is the pearl of great price. Have you discovered that pearl yet? If you have, can you sense how He is pursuing you now? What purposes does He have for you? If you haven't discovered it yet, please keep reading!

*O God, I have tasted Thy goodness, and it has both satisfied me and made me thirsty for more. I am painfully conscious of my need for further grace.*

*I am ashamed of my lack of desire. O God, the Triune God, I want to want Thee; I long to be filled with longing; I thirst to be made more thirsty still.*

*Show me Thy glory, I pray Thee, so that I may know Thee indeed. Begin in mercy a new work of love within me. Say*

*to my soul, "Rise up my love, my fair one, and come away."*
*Then give me grace to rise and follow Thee up from this misty*
*lowland where I have wandered so long.*[9]

—A.W. Tozer

"The LORD would speak to Moses face to face, as one speaks to a friend."

Exodus 33:11

# CHAPTER 2

# The Intimate, Holy One

The story is told by the Persians of the great Shah Abbas, who reigned magnificently in Persia, but loved to mingle with the people in disguise. Once, dressed as a poor man, he descended the long flight of stairs, dark and damp, to the tiny cellar where the fireman, seated on ashes, was tending the furnace.

The Shah sat down beside him and began to talk. At mealtime the fireman produced some coarse, black bread and a jug of water and they ate and drank. The Shah went away, but returned again and again, for his heart was filled with sympathy for the lonely man. He gave his sweet counsel, and the poor man opened his whole heart and loved this friend, so kind, so wise, and yet poor like himself.

At last the emperor thought, "I will tell him who I am, and see what gift he will ask." So he said, "You think me poor, but I am Shah Abbas your emperor." He expected a petition for some great thing, but the man sat silent. Gazing, he said, "Haven't you understood? I can make you rich and noble, can give you a city, can appoint you as a great ruler. Have you nothing to ask?"

The man replied gently, "Yes, my lord, I understood. But what *is this you have done, to leave your palace and glory, to sit with me in this dark place, to partake of my coarse fare, to care whether my heart is glad or sorry? Even you can give nothing more precious. On others you may bestow rich presents but to me you have given yourself; it only remains to ask that you never withdraw this gift of your friendship."[1]*

This poor man had learned a key lesson, as did the Shah. Friendship is the most precious gift of all, especially when it's deep and intimate. This intimate kind of relationship is what I believe Moses shared with God. They were friends. And it was a deep, rich friendship that became stronger over time as they weathered one difficulty after another. Together they would lead more than a million people out of Egypt, through the Red Sea, through the wilderness, and finally to the promised land. Moses would meet with God and be so filled with His presence that his face shone brightly as it reflected the glory and majesty of God.

Moses is a model for us of what friendship with God means. It means that God gets to lead our lives, just as He did with Moses for forty years through the wilderness. It's every day when we wake up and our feet hit the floor, making a choice to live for Him. He writes the story of our lives—and when it's all done, and we come to the end of our journey, what a joy it would be if others could say that we reflected the glory and majesty of God. That we act like Him. That our lives have been shaped by Him.

## GOD IS SOVEREIGN

Abraham's descendants, the Israelites, went to Egypt during a time of great famine. They were able to work freely as sheep-herders until a new pharaoh in Egypt took them into slavery.[2]

This was a part of God's promise to Abraham, that his people would be slaves for four hundred years and then God would deliver them. Moses was the man that God used to deliver them.

Moses was born during a time of great oppression for the Israelites. The pharaoh, alarmed at how numerous the Israelites were becoming, ordered midwives to kill every Hebrew baby boy at birth. Those who were not killed at birth were to be thrown into the Nile River to die, according to his command. But God had other plans for Moses. And in His plan, His sovereignty is revealed. He is the God who seeks. He is the God who keeps His promises. And He is also the God who always accomplishes His purposes. I love that about God. He can do whatever He chooses to do, and nothing and no one can stop His plan.

Moses's mother took him to the Nile River, placing him in a reed basket that would float on the water. When Pharaoh's daughter went to the river to bathe, she heard the baby crying and sent her maid to get him. One look at the beautiful baby and she was captivated. She sent for one of the Hebrew women to take care of him. The woman turned out to be Moses's mother. So Moses was nursed and weaned by his own mother, and he grew up in Pharaoh's palace, being groomed for leadership.

## GOD CHOOSES FOR HIS PURPOSES

I believe that God loves to do that! Moses had no business being in the pharaoh's palace. He was a Hebrew. He was born a slave. He had the sentence of death on him. But God defied all that in order to accomplish His purposes. God chooses leaders. Often they are unlikely by the world's standards. I imagine it was unsettling for Moses, especially in light of the fact that he

HE CALLS ME FRIEND

was not a good speaker, to see himself as the leader of more than a million people.

I think of that often when I find myself standing before hundreds, or even thousands, of people sharing my story, talking about love and justice and reconciliation, talking about friendship and the gospel. With only a fifth-grade education, I have no business standing in those places, talking to people who have high titles and impressive resumes. In the early years, that was something that I really struggled with; I felt inadequate and out of place. And I still feel some of that even now, after all these years. But now I'm trying to turn that insecurity into gratitude and into thankfulness that God chooses to use me still.

> God somehow makes a way for those of us who are weak by the world's standards.

God somehow makes a way for those of us who are weak by the world's standards. He can make much of a life if it's committed to Him. The song "Ordinary People" stresses that God loves using plain old ordinary people: "Little becomes much when you place it in the Master's hand."[3]

Even though Moses had been raised in a privileged environment, he still identified with his people, the Israelites. Moses's actions help us know how to address the issue of privilege in our day. It has become a really controversial topic. Moses had all kinds of privilege: wealth, power, and prestige, but he gave it all up to help those who were helpless and unable to defend themselves. He identified with those who were suffering, so that their pain became his pain. They were in slavery and suffering more and more each day, and one day he saw an Egyptian beating a Hebrew. He retaliated by killing the Egyptian, and was forced to run for his life. He went to Midian and for forty years tended sheep.

But God was about to draw Moses to friendship and relationship, and to His purposes for his life. The Hound of Heaven was about to capture His prey.

## GOD DESIRES TO BE KNOWN

God appeared to Moses in a burning bush. Moses noticed that even though the bush was on fire it wasn't being consumed. It continuously burned. Moses went to examine the bush, and God allowed him to come close, but then said, "Do not come any closer. . . . Take off your sandals, for the place where you are standing is holy ground. . . . I am the God of your father, the God of Abraham, the God of Isaac and the God of Jacob" (Ex. 3:5–6).

This is a glorious picture of God. He allowed Moses to come close, but then He commanded him to take off his shoes. This balance of coming close and taking off our shoes is beautiful. God desires closeness. He wants to be known. A key part of friendship is to know the other. God has done His part in helping us know Him. We could know nothing about Him if He hadn't moved on the hearts of men to write His story. All of Scripture, from Genesis to Revelation, is the self-revelation of God—who He is, what He thinks, what He desires.

The first time I read all the way through the Bible, I was amazed at how awesome God is. He had a purpose from the very beginning, and in His sovereignty He accomplishes everything that He set out to do. He created people to have fellowship with Him. Even before we sinned, God had a plan to draw us back into fellowship with Him. His desire for fellowship with fallen humans was so strong that He was willing to die to bring us back to a loving relationship with Himself. And in the end He will have eternal friendship and fellowship with everyone who chooses to be with Him. That's the broad outline of His story, but it's when we examine how He interacted with people like Moses that we get a deeper understanding of who God is.

It makes me sad to think that so few people take advantage of knowing Him by reading the Bible. According to a study, "Americans have a positive view of the Bible. And many say the Christian scriptures are filled with moral lessons for today. However, more than half of Americans have read little or none of the Bible."[4]

Maybe I'm just old-fashioned, but I keep my Bible close at hand. It's like a love letter from a friend. When you get a love letter, you want to read it again and again. You pay attention to every word. You notice the punctuation. You read every line and you read between the lines. I think this is how we should want to read His love letter to us. Every time I pick it up I learn more and more about Him. More about His love for me. More about His purposes for me. When we really love God we love His Word, because we know that His Word is His heart and His message to us. God had a face-to-face friendship with Moses and, because of His Spirit within us, we can have a face-to-face friendship with Him by reading His Word. It's how we come to know Him.

This idea of being known to the other is powerful. It's the basis for true friendship and it can't happen without time spent together. Vera Mae and I decided that we really wanted and needed to put forth effort to get to know our great-grandchildren. We don't want to leave this earth without them knowing us and understanding how much we love them. So my grandson said that he was going to start bringing them over on Monday nights to play hide-and-seek in this big old house. There are so many closets and cabinets they can hide in. They get so excited! They run and hide and I try my best to find them. I get down on the floor to play with them. When they get ready to leave, they crawl up in the bed with Momma and they kiss her. They love it. They're getting to know us and we're getting to know them. I try my best to out-love them. I'm having fun making myself known to them. I think that God wants us to get to know Him like that. He wants us to enjoy getting to know Him.

## GOD IS HOLY

God's command to Moses to take off his shoes points to the truth that He is holy. He is set apart from everything and everyone else. There is no other God like our God! Moses is coming to see that he should not be there, that this God is holy and that this God—who the angels stand in the presence of —has come to be his friend. And he is struck by the truth that this holy and awesome God would take a raggedy sinner into loving relationship. He is humbled and full of gratitude.

Friendship with God and gratitude. They go together. That's our weakness today. We don't have the right kind of gratitude toward God for choosing to be friends with us. We have cooled down in the face of this awesome God and He has become just another guy. We have made Him into a man, and our hearts toward Him have become lukewarm. We have lost an awareness of who He is. He is not the big guy or a higher power. He is not the man upstairs. He's more than that. He is holy.

Holy, holy, holy! Lord God Almighty!
Early in the morning our song shall rise to Thee;
. . . . . . . . . . .

Only Thou art holy; there is none beside Thee,
Perfect in pow'r, in love, and purity.[5]

Moses understood this idea of God's holiness as he came to know Him as friend: "Who among the gods is like you, LORD? Who is like you—majestic in holiness, awesome in glory, working wonders?" (Ex. 15:11).

During the journey from Egypt to the promised land, Moses encountered God on a daily basis. He came to know Him as the God of deliverance when He miraculously opened up the Red Sea and allowed the people of Israel to walk across on dry land. He came to know Him as the God who provides when he looked out on the ground early every morning and saw manna from heaven that God used to feed them on their wilderness journey. But no encounter with God was as intimate as what he experienced at the Tent of Meeting, described in Exodus 33:7–11a:

> Now Moses used to take a tent and pitch it outside the
> camp some distance away, calling it the "tent of meeting."
> Anyone inquiring of the LORD would go to the tent of
> meeting outside the camp. And whenever Moses went out
> to the tent, all the people rose and stood at the entrances
> to their tents, watching Moses until he entered the tent.
> As Moses went into the tent, the pillar of cloud would
> come down and stay at the entrance, while the LORD spoke
> with Moses. Whenever the people saw the pillar of cloud
> standing at the entrance to the tent, they all stood and
> worshiped, each at the entrance to their tent. *The LORD*
> *would speak to Moses face to face, as one speaks to a friend.*

## BECOMING MORE AND MORE LIKE HIM

Moses was changed by the intimacy of his relationship with God. After time spent with God, his face shone—it reflected the glory of God. He had to cover his face because it frightened the people. Our friendship with God should change us too, in a way that is obvious to those who are around us. God's standard for His friends is this: "Be holy because I, the LORD your God, am holy" (Lev. 19:2). This doesn't mean that we are to be perfect. God is the only one who is perfect. But we are to be growing and looking more like Him. Confessing our sins and receiving His forgiveness and His righteousness. It means growing in how we love others. Obeying Him when He's nudging us to love people who we don't want to love. Growing in how we are forgiving and patient with others.

Wanting to be like Him should lead us to friendship and right relationships with others. If we say we know God and hate another person, we are not holy. If I don't like people who don't look like me, I haven't spent enough time with Him. We are growing in our holiness when we are in communion with God and with one another. My prayer is that I am changing day by day to look more like Him. I'm learning that I must spend time with Him for that to happen.

> The eagle is built for a solitary life. There is no bird so alone; other birds go in flocks—the eagle never, two at most together, and they are mates. Its majesty consists partly in its solitariness. It lives apart because other birds cannot live where and as it lives, and follow where it leads. The true child of God must consent to a lonely life apart with God, and often the condition of holiness is separation.[6]

I don't believe that God wants us to separate ourselves entirely from the world, to live like certain religious orders, secluded and meditating all day every day. But He does expect us to separate ourselves from those persons and things that pull us away from the life He's calling us to. I don't know if I would have been able to hear God's call without leaving Mississippi the first time. I needed to get away from the negative influences that pulled me down and kept me just a few steps ahead of the law. Being set apart for God can mean having to be careful about who we choose to be friends with.

> "A mirror reflects a man's face, but what he is really like is shown by the kind of friends he chooses."[7]
> —Colin Powell

## GOD IS A MERCIFUL FRIEND

Toward the end of his life, Moses had been leading the people of Israel for many years. I suppose he got frustrated with them and their constant complaining. So when God told him to speak to the rock and that water would flow so that the people could drink, Moses disobeyed God's command. Instead of speaking to the rock, he spoke sharply to the people and struck the rock (Num. 20:8–11). God punished Moses for his disobedience by refusing to allow him to go into the promised land. Once again God demonstrated that while He desires intimate, close fellowship, He also demands obedience. But in His mercy He allowed Moses to look over into the promised land to see the beautiful place that the people of Israel would enter into.

Moses's impatience and pride got the best of him and prevented him from enjoying the fruit of his labor after forty years in the wilderness. I believe that we all struggle with pride in some form. I wonder if the health issues I've been dealing with are God's way of keeping my pride in check. My health has been almost like a thorn in the flesh, constantly reminding me that I am frail, that without Him I am nothing, and I have limited time to accomplish what He called me to do.

Yet in His mercy He has allowed me to look over into the promised land. A short while ago I was privileged to speak at Stone Mountain, Georgia. Stone Mountain has a difficult history. It was the place of the rebirth of the Ku Klux Klan in 1915, as crosses were burned at the summit. And the United Daughters of the Confederacy commissioned a carving of Confederate figures on the gray dome. For the next fifty years, Labor Day cross burnings were held at the site.

> **God led. Moses followed. How is He leading you day by day? Are you spending time with Him and coming to know Him better each day?**

God transformed that location and birthed a new movement based on prayer—the OneRace Gathering—as twenty thousand millennials and others, who are tired of the ethnic strife and division in our country, came together.[8] At the summit of the mountain they asked me to pray a prayer over the young people who are taking on the banner of reconciliation and boldly continuing the fight. Their leader asked me to pray a generational blessing over them, and I imagine it must have felt something like that for Moses to give his parting words to Joshua, who would take his place in leading the people of Israel into the promised land.

I was so moved to have that privilege, and I felt God's presence as I opened my mouth to pray:

"Oh God of heaven, the God of the heavens and the earth, we stand on this rock. And, Lord, together we can say on this solid rock—on Jesus our Savior—on this solid rock we stand. And we can say all other ground is sinking sand! Lord, I thank You for this generation. I thank You that they are listening to Your voice. And they're hearing Your voice. They're bringing their loneliness. They're bringing their pain to You. They're passionate. Entering into another's pain. Oh Lord, bless this generation. This is their day. I have lived to see this. I have longed for this! Our forefathers have longed for this. So bless this millennial generation. Encourage them! Let them go into the marketplace. Let them bring lost souls into the local congregation and disciple them, so they can go out and we can reach the world together. Oh, bless this generation! Be with them! Guide them! In Jesus' name!"

It was one of God's tenderest mercies to allow me to live long enough to see those thousands of young people excited to take the reconciliation and friendship message to a lost world. When we came down from the mountain, I was able to share with them that leadership is not a position, it's a calling. God calls leaders of His own choosing. We cannot afford to sit and wait for someone to give us a position in order for us to serve. A lot of times young men are put into training for how to be a deacon. I think that's good . . . but it's not the final word. This is skills development. But the call of God is hearing deeper. It's a deeper call. It's a call for a lifetime that makes you leave everything else behind to run after that call. We must obey God's call at all cost.

God's friendship with Moses showed the day-by-day leading and following that marked their relationship. God led. Moses followed. How is He leading you day by day? Are you spending time with Him and coming to know Him better each day?

God calls each of His friends into intimate, face-to-face fellowship with Him and faithful obedience to His commands. He is the friend who desires to be known, and He is holy. Like the Shah of Abbas, He sits and communes with us along the journey of life. To know Him as friend is the greatest gift of all. If He is your friend, you will never walk alone. These words written by my son Phillip help say it best:[9]

> He calls me friend. . . .
> He is a friend like no other,
> with Him I'll never walk alone.
> He never criticizes the hopeless,
> He'll gently walk me safely home.
> He calls me friend . . . He is the Alpha and
> Omega, what He has said, that's what He'll do.
> He never says He will not help me,
> His precious Word is ever true.
> He calls me friend.

"After removing Saul, he made David their king. God testified concerning him: 'I have found David son of Jesse, a man after my own heart; he will do everything I want him to do.'"

Acts 13:22

# CHAPTER 3

# The Great Forgiver

*Two friends were walking through the desert. During some point of the journey, they had an argument, and one friend slapped the other one in the face.*

*The one who got slapped was hurt, but without saying anything, wrote in the sand, "Today my best friend slapped me in the face."*

*They kept on walking until they found an oasis, where they decided to take a bath. The one who had been slapped got stuck in the mire and started drowning, but the friend saved him. After he recovered from the near drowning, he wrote on a stone "Today my best friend saved my life."*

*The friend who had slapped and saved his best friend asked him, "After I hurt you, you wrote in the sand and now, you write on a stone, why?" The other friend replied, "When someone hurts us we should write it down in the sand where winds of forgiveness can erase it away. But when someone does something good for us, we must engrave it in stone where no wind can ever erase it."*[1]

Forgiveness is a big deal, and you can't really have a true friendship without it. To be human is to fail. We make mistakes. We hurt one another. To forgive is to make a decision to cancel a debt that you are owed and not to hold it against your offender. I'm glad that when we offend God He writes it in the sand where the winds of forgiveness can erase it. I learned a lot about that from David's story. It gave me so much hope. If God could forgive and continue to be friends with David, then surely He would forgive me for my past and for the things I do day after day that grieve His heart.

## GOD CHOOSES A SINNER

David was another one of God's unlikely leaders. He was the youngest and smallest of Jesse's sons. When the prophet Samuel came to visit Jesse with a message that God had sent him to choose one of his sons and anoint him, the expectation was that it would surely be one of the tall, good-looking young men. (You can read about this in 1 Samuel 16:1–13.) But Samuel passed over all of them, and set his eyes on David, the scrawny shepherd boy. David would make a name for himself when he killed the giant Goliath and went into battle victorious. He was God's choice for king.

But a wandering eye proved to be a weakness for David. After he became king he decided to stay back home while his army was at battle. From the rooftop of the palace he saw the beautiful Bathsheba and sent for her. He spent the night with her, and later she sent word that she was pregnant. He schemed to cover up his sin by calling her husband, Uriah, back from the front lines, assuming he would be glad to spend the night with his wife so people would think the pregnancy was a result of their union. David's plan was unsuccessful. The husband proved to be a much more honorable man than David was and did not take advantage of the chance to be with his wife while his fellow soldiers were away at war. So David sent him into a position in the battle where he was sure to be killed, and he was. David took his wife, Bathsheba, as his own.

God judged David's sin by taking the life of the baby. And that really should end the story of David. If I were writing his story, I'd probably just end it right there. From a human perspective, David's sin was too gross for him to be friends with God and make it into heaven. And if David was any other man, his story might have ended there. But David showed what was in his heart by what he did next. He cried out to the God of heaven pleading for forgiveness:

> Have mercy on me, O God,
>     according to your unfailing love;
> according to your great compassion
>     blot out my transgressions.
> Wash away all my iniquity
>     and cleanse me from my sin.
>
> For I know my transgressions,
>     and my sin is always before me.
> Against you, you only, have I sinned
>     and done what is evil in your sight;
> so you are right in your verdict
>     and justified when you judge.
> —Psalm 51:1–4

That was David's brokenness over his sin. He was broken and contrite. He was crushed in his spirit to think that he had done something so vile against another human being. He had used his power to take advantage of another person; and he had compounded that sin by killing an innocent man. He understood that a sin against any person is a sin against God.

> **There have been valleys of anger and disobedience when I felt far, far from Him. Yet every time I cried out to Him, He was there. He took me back. That's what friendship with God looks like.**

And he was desperate to be right with God again. At the same time, he was humbled to think that he could ever be right again with a holy God because of the things he had done. This is the beauty of brokenness. It is a tool that God uses to draw us back to Himself.

David's brokenness over his sin is a model for us. I'm afraid that we've lost a sense of shame and regret over our sin. We rarely even use the word "sin" anymore. We talk about making mistakes, coming up short, telling white lies. But God calls it all sin and it grieves His heart, and while it does not change His unconditional love for us, it does disturb our fellowship and friendship. But when we acknowledge our sin and cry out to Him, He forgives. As Francis Chan puts it, that's crazy love! He writes our sin in the sand where the winds of forgiveness can wash it away!

When Vera Mae and I read the story of David together, I began to feel and remember those sins that I committed after we first got married. There was a period of time early on, right after I came back from the army, when I wasn't acting like a husband should. I was unfaithful. I was not true to my vows, and my actions brought Vera Mae so much pain. Just reading the story called my sins back into my memory. I grieved them all over again. Vera Mae forgave me and committed herself to loving me as a wife does her husband. I still think about that now, especially in these last days as I get to take care of her. It is an undeserved privilege. This is the point where I connect with David the most. I wake up every morning grateful that God would love me in spite of my past. That He would be my friend in spite of the fact that I continue to sin. I'm almost afraid that I will take His love and His friendship for granted, and I don't ever want to do that.

## GOD FORGIVES THE REPENTANT SINNER

Andraé Crouch knew something about this sense of brokenness when our sin takes us into a faraway land. His song "Take Me Back" is beautiful in expressing what it feels like when our friendship with God is broken:

> *I feel that I'm so far from you Lord*
> *But still I hear you calling me*
> *Those simple things that I once knew*
> *Their memories keep drawing me.*
> *I must confess, Lord I've been blessed*
> *But yet my soul's not satisfied.*
> *Renew my faith, restore my joy*
> *And dry my weeping eyes. . . .*
> *Take me back, take me back dear*
> *Lord to the place where I*
> *first received you.*[2]

That song comes from a place of brokenness. It's a cry for forgiveness. For God to take us back to that place of close friendship and fellowship with Him. It should be our heart cry whenever we find ourselves in a distant land carried away by our sin. It's been the cry of my heart again and again over my long years of knowing the Lord. There have been valleys of anger and disobedience when I felt far, far from Him. Yet every time I cried out to Him, He was there. He took me back. That's what friendship with God looks like. It's knowing that no matter how far we wander into that faraway land, He is waiting with open arms to take us back and to forgive. He is the God who forgives.

Once President Lincoln was asked how he was going to treat the rebellious Southerners when they had finally been defeated and returned to the Union of the United States. The questioner expected that Lincoln would take a dire vengeance, but he answered, "I will treat them as if they had never been away."[3]

God is like that. When He forgives, He treats us like we never messed up. He casts our sins into the sea of forgetfulness and puts up a "no fishing" sign there.

Henri Nouwen said this about forgiveness: "There are two sides to forgiveness: giving and receiving. Although at first sight giving seems to be harder, it often appears that we are not able to offer forgiveness to others because we have not been able fully to receive it. Only as people who have accepted forgiveness can we find the inner freedom to give it."[4]

We can't really give forgiveness until we have received it from God. And we can't receive forgiveness from Him until we are broken and contrite in heart.

## ANOTHER SIDE OF FORGIVENESS

When we are forgiven by God, we must accept forgiveness from Him and from others who offer it—that's another side of forgiveness. We know from Scripture that David learned this lesson. He was forced to flee because his son Absalom challenged him for the throne. As he fled from Jerusalem, Shimei (a relative of Saul) cursed him and told him that he deserved to be run from his kingdom (see 2 Sam. 16:5–13). It was unthinkable that anyone would talk to the king like this. David could have had him killed on the spot for those remarks. But David chose to spare his life because he understood the sovereignty of God. "Leave him alone; let him curse, for the LORD has told him to. It may be that the LORD will look upon my misery and restore to me his covenant blessing instead of his curse today" (vv. 11b–12).

But when Absalom had been killed and David was returning in victory to reclaim his rightful position on the throne, it was Shimei who met him on the way and asked for forgiveness (vv. 16–23). When David's men suggested that Shimei should die because he had cursed David, David said to Shimei, "You shall not die." David had learned the lesson of forgiveness. Those who have been forgiven much should be ready to give forgiveness freely.

I think about that a lot today. I suppose that is what has fueled my zeal to love everybody. I remember the heavy weight of anger and bitterness I carried. I was angry about being mistreated just because of the color of my skin. I was angry about what happened to my brother Clyde. I was angry about the systems at work in Mississippi that kept my people at a substandard level of living. I was angry. And it was a deep, abiding anger. It would either explode and destroy me and everybody around me—or God would have to take it away and show me how to move forward. He did that for me. He forgave me of my thoughts of taking revenge and getting even. He forgave me for all of it. And He showed me how to channel that energy into work that would please Him.

That was many years ago. And I'm full of gratitude that the Lord did that in my heart. But the truth is that He has had to continue that work in my heart again and again. When I hear about mistreatment of people and see the wrong that is taking place right in front of my eyes, I have to take the anger back to Him. And I have to forgive those who are doing the mistreating, because I have been forgiven much.

My friends say that I've been talking about dying for the last forty years and they laugh. I think I'm finding that God wants us to live with this death of the old man. When the apostle Paul said he had to "die daily,"[5] I think this is what he was talking about. I don't want my old thoughts. I need to remind myself daily that I've died to that old self who harbored anger and hatred. I rejoice in knowing that He has forgiven me. But His forgiveness scares me. I'm afraid that I might start sinning knowing that He's so gracious. We've got to live within that tension.

That may be what's missing today. There's so much anger. Everybody seems to be angry about something or other. We're expressing that anger in words that destroy and in actions that divide. We're sinning and covering up our sin instead of confessing it. We have become victimized by our own unforgiveness. We're doing this as individuals and as a nation. And our hearts have become stony and hard, holding all that anger and sin inside. God is the friend who can handle all our anger. He can heal our hurts and give us purpose and direction. But we must become broken over our sin, as David did.

## GOD IS THE GOOD SHEPHERD

In David's brokenness he cried out to God to forgive him. I believe that God always answers that prayer. And when He answered David's prayer for Him to restore his joy, David came to know Him in a way that few people can claim. He came to know God as a Shepherd. He learned a lot about friendship with God along the way. His twenty-third psalm is a guide to who God is for His friends:

The LORD is my shepherd, I lack nothing.
    He makes me lie down in green pastures,
he leads me beside quiet waters,
    he refreshes my soul.
He guides me along the right paths
    for his name's sake.
Even though I walk
    through the darkest valley,
I will fear no evil,
    for you are with me;
your rod and your staff,
    they comfort me.

You prepare a table before me
    in the presence of my enemies.
You anoint my head with oil;
    my cup overflows.
Surely your goodness and love will follow me
    all the days of my life,
and I will dwell in the house of the LORD
    forever.

When I read the words of that psalm, I knew that David knew God intimately. He used a metaphor to describe God that he was very familiar with. David knew what it meant to be a shepherd. He had cared for his father's sheep in Bethlehem. He had protected them from the lion and the bear. And he knew what sheep are like. Sheep have been described as unintelligent animals. They need someone to take care of them at all times. They cannot defend themselves. They need to be led to pastures to eat and to clean water to drink. If one jumps off a cliff, all the rest follow. If they get lost, they can't find their way back. As a shepherd, David would carry a rod and a staff to rescue them if one would fall into a crag or over a cliff.

Sheep are helpless. But they are unique because they know the voice of their shepherd. It's common in nomadic cultures for flocks of sheep to intermingle. But when the shepherd calls, his own sheep will answer. I imagine that God referred to His people as sheep because He wanted us to always remember that we are dependent on Him for everything. He is our shepherd. He is the one who charts our path for us because we do not know which way to go. David's path to becoming king was littered with seasons spent running for his life away from Saul, and later, running from his son, who sought to overthrow his kingship. Yet it was these difficulties along his way that helped him to know God as the friend who is a shepherd.

If it had been left up to me, I certainly would have never returned to Mississippi to live. But He knew that was where I needed to be in order to obey His calling on my life. He is the shepherd who leads. He is able to lead us even through the valley of the shadow of death and keep us safe from all harm.

David was known as the greatest king of Israel. He was a leader, and his example shows us what godly leadership should look like. Not perfect. But trying to please Him. And when failure comes, as it always does, the godly leader acknowledges his sin and cries out to God for forgiveness.

I am constantly reminded of just how much I need this Shepherd. And I'm also reminded of how much my life should be marked by forgiveness. I owe a debt of forgiveness to everyone who has hurt me. Are there persons He is leading you to forgive? He can help you do that.

Bruce Larson tells about a cartoon that appeared in the *New Yorker*. "This is the fourth time we've killed the fatted calf," a frustrated father says to his prodigal son.[6] But doesn't God do this again and again for us? I am grateful that God doesn't become frustrated or angry when I come back seeking forgiveness for a sinful thought or action. He keeps killing the fatted calf and He keeps writing in the sand so the winds of forgiveness can blow them away.

I've learned a lot about true friendship by watching how God interacted with Abraham, Moses, and David. God is a pursuer. He goes after those He sets His heart on for friendship. God is holy, but He wants face-to-face friendship with us. He wants to be close to us. And God forgives even the worst of sinners. He forgives and He doesn't hold our sin against us. He's that kind of friend, and He shows us what true friendship looks like.

I consider my wife and my friends to be God's greatest gifts to me. God has used them to strengthen and to encourage me along my journey. One of those special friends is Ken Smith. God brought us together many years ago, and one of the things that I have learned from my friendship with Ken is that friendship is forever. I'll let Ken share in his own words.

Let's Hear It from Ken Smith:

# *Friendship*
# IS FOREVER

My dear friend John Perkins has asked me to reflect on our friendship. This is a great joy for me since our friendship is a precious link in my walk with Christ. My friendship with John started in a most peculiar way, and God's plan for the depth of that was unknown to me for quite some time.

I was attending a CCDA conference (Christian Community Development Association) being held at Moody Bible Institute. Each morning there was an eight o'clock Bible study and the teacher was John Perkins. One evening I talked briefly with John, but it was a short conversation with no real substance. However, on the next morning after this brief encounter, I was sitting in the front row waiting for this wonderful time of teaching to begin, when John came lumbering across the stage area, approached me, and said, "Ken, how are you this morning? Will you be my friend?"

I responded, "Sure, I will be your friend."

To which John responded, "I mean forever!"

Now I know that it was God's perfect will that these words were spoken because they served as a kind of tether, or anchor, to keep me from drifting away from this relational commitment to be John's friend forever. One of the things my father had taught me was not to forget my commitments to others, and it is only now, in looking back, that I can see the value of his training.

I had some contact with John after this time, but eventually we lost contact with each other for a number of years. But one day when I was at a deep point of despair, God prompted me to call John. When John answered the phone and I announced myself, he said, "Is this Ken Smith from Des Moines? Where have you been, brother? I have not heard from you forever!"

So clear was the message from the Holy Spirit in this simple but loving conversation between two seekers of Jesus that it would be the start of a friendship so deep and meaningful that it would change the course of my life and help me understand what God desires between us and Him; true friendship that will be forever!

One of the things that defines our friendship is our mutual passion for knowing the truth and being free; in other words, experiencing life to the fullest. What a wonderful privilege it has been to have this relationship and the understanding that has come with it.

I think friendship should be defined both by what it is and by what it is not. It is a longing of the heart for something that cannot be filled by anything other than friendship. True friendship is not something that needs to be reassured every day; instead it is a deep assurance of relationship that can be trusted and counted on no matter the circumstances or challenges involved.

Friendship is deeply rooted in transparency and honesty. It stands on the common ground of brokenness and forgiveness. It is lasting, not temporary. Friendship is life itself—real life. It lasts forever.

I've often pondered this question: Why would the Lord allow me time and presence with a man that He has used in His kingdom work in such a way? He is recognized for such God-given wisdom and has received sixteen honorary doctorates. What do I have to offer this man that could somehow justify our time together?

Well, now I know. It is so I can share in his sorrow when he has pain, so I can eat meals with him in the presence of friends, so I can support him in his calling to tell others the good news of Jesus' sacrifice and that we can be reconciled together in Him, so I can join in with his personal family and feel the joy of being accepted and loved by them, so I can get a vision for this need to build Christ-centered communities and then sup-port those who have heard the message God has called John to declare and are working hard to live it out. I can laugh and rejoice with him, and I can share the gifts God has allowed me to enjoy and see him enjoy them too. I could continue the list, but it adds up to this: so I can be his friend as he is my friend, as he shares all of his gifts with me and I share my gifts with him, so together we can relish and grow in the friendship we have with God through Jesus Christ.

"Will you be my friend forever?" In essence, this is what Jesus, our Messiah and Savior, is offering, and this is what John and I share together. And if we can find great joy in sitting on the back porch at my ranch in Montana admiring the beauty of creation and glorifying God in it, then what awaits us in the completion of this friendship?

What a great privilege it has been, and is, to be a part of this friendship and to look forward to all that God will do through it in the days ahead.

Thank you, Brother John, for being my friend. I love you very much!

Ken Smith
*Ken is a real estate investor who makes his home in Urbandale, Iowa.*

*Part Two*

# FRIENDSHIP
# WITH JESUS

"If not for Your mercy, Lord, my sin would overwhelm me and separate me from You. I am amazed at how You have turned my broken life into something You can use for Your glory."

———

Ruth Bell Graham

# CHAPTER 4

# The God Who Came to Us

*One raw winter night a man heard a thumping sound against the kitchen storm door. He went to the window and watched as tiny, shivering sparrows, attracted to the evident warmth inside, beat in vain against the glass.*

*Touched, the farmer bundled up and trudged through the fresh snow to open the barn for the struggling birds. He turned on the lights, tossed some hay in a corner, and sprinkled a trail of saltine crackers to direct them to the barn. But the sparrows, which had scattered in all directions when he emerged from the house, still hid in the darkness, afraid of him. He tried various tactics. . . . Nothing worked. He, a huge alien creature, had terrified them; the birds could not understand that he actually desired to help.*

*He withdrew to his house and watched the doomed sparrows through a window. As he stared, a thought hit him like lightning from a clear blue sky:* If only I could become a bird—one of them—just for a moment. Then I wouldn't frighten them so. I could show them the way to warmth and safety. . . . *A man's becoming a bird is nothing compared to God's becoming a man. The concept of a sovereign being as big as the universe He created, confining Himself to a human body was—and is—too much for some people to believe.*[1]

But He did it. The great God in heaven came in the form of a human being to fix our relationship problem. We call this the incarnation. The incarnation brought Him out of eternity and put flesh on Him.

We were doomed just as the sparrows were. But God decided to come to us in the form of a man. Jesus was the One who was spoken of in the garden of Eden when Adam and Eve sinned and had to be sent out, never to return again. When God told the serpent that the offspring of the woman would crush his head, He was speaking of Jesus (Gen. 3:15). Jesus was the God-man. He was God in the flesh who came to earth to fix what had been broken in the garden of Eden.

## THE SIN PROBLEM

In the garden, Adam and Eve had face-to-face communion with God before they sinned. But sin broke the fellowship. And from that point on, God's people had to offer sacrifices for their sins in order to restore fellowship with God. God provided the Ten Commandments to let His people know what He expected them to do; how they were to live. But no one was able to live without breaking those rules.

All the Old Testament people of God looked forward to the day when someone would come who would be able to satisfy God's commands to live without sin. They honored Abraham as the father of the faith, but they knew that he sinned. At least two times he lied and said that Sarah was his sister in order to protect himself and to save his life. They loved Moses for leading them through the wilderness and to the promised land, but they remembered that he struck the rock and wasn't permitted to enter in. And everyone knew about David's sin with Bathsheba. It was clear that no one could live without sin. So Abraham offered sacrifices, Moses offered sacrifices, and David offered sacrifices (Gen. 22:13; Ex. 29:42; 2 Sam. 6:13). Sin required a sacrifice. And the sacrifices had to be offered repeatedly.

Once a year on the Day of Atonement all the people of Israel would gather, and the priest would bring two goats. One would be sacrificed to pay for the sins of the people and the other would be set free.

> "When Aaron has finished making atonement for the Most Holy Place, the tent of meeting and the altar, he shall bring forward the live goat. He is to lay both hands on the head of the live goat and confess over it all the wickedness and rebellion of the Israelites—all their sins—and put them on the goat's head. He shall send the goat away into the wilderness in the care of someone appointed for the task. The goat will carry on itself all their sins to a remote place; and the man shall release it in the wilderness." —Leviticus 16:20–22

This goat was known as the scapegoat and he represented the One who would take away the sins of the world. That One was Jesus. He would come and be the ultimate sacrifice for sin so that there would no longer be a need to sacrifice goats and sheep and pigeons. He would give His life so that broken friendship and fellowship with God could be finally restored.

## GOD—BORN IN A MANGER

In the fullness of time, God broke into history as a baby in a manger. That blows my mind. The God of creation, who is all powerful, sovereign, holy, eternal, and so much more, chose to come to earth as a helpless baby born to a poor virgin who was espoused to a carpenter. It's no wonder that friendship with God requires humility. His humbling Himself to such a low estate should motivate us to respond in humility to Him and to others.

Humility is hard to come by these days. It's not a desirable quality in a culture that promotes pride and power. What is humility? "Humility is perfect quietness of heart. It is to expect nothing, to wonder at nothing that is done to me, to feel nothing done against me. It is to be at rest when nobody praises me, and when I am blamed or despised. It is to have a blessed home in the Lord, where I can go in and shut the door, and kneel to my Father in secret, and am at peace as in a deep sea of calmness, when all around and above is trouble."[2]

My friend Dr. Tony Evans says that, "in football, they tell the offensive line, no matter how big you are, stay low. So that you can have leverage, stay low. No matter how big you get in life, stay low. No matter what title you have in front of your name, how much money you have in the bank, or how many people know who you are, stay low. The moment you use your knowledge, prestige, power, or resources to attempt to be like God, it will be made very clear, very soon, that there is only one God. Humble yourself beneath His mighty hand."[3]

I like that definition of humility . . . stay low. That's what God did when He clothed Himself in flesh and came to live among us. The baby born in a manger came to show us how to live without sin, and ultimately to die for our sins. He would live a life that was holy. He was constantly reminding others that He had to be about His Father's business. He was obedient to God in all things. And He invited everyone to be His friends. "Come to me, all you who are weary and burdened, and I will give you rest. Take my yoke upon you and learn from me, for I am gentle and humble in heart, and you will find rest for your souls" (Matt. 11:28–29).

## THE GOD WHO CARRIES OUR BURDENS

When Jesus invites us to be yoked up with Him, it's an invitation to friendship. When you put oxen into a yoke, its purpose is to help the animals pull the load together. When they hear the sound of the whip, they jerk forward and pull the load. When you yoke up with Jesus, He pulls the load with you. The crack of the whip is His voice. "I call My own sheep by name. They know Me." With Jesus we pull together when we hear His voice. We can carry an unlimited amount of trouble, trial, and stress when we are yoked up and become friends with Jesus. We are never alone. For the rest of life we will never walk alone.

So many people are living under a heavy burden and need to know that Jesus will carry that burden and will get in the yoke with them. I preached a message at a church in Pennsylvania not long ago. I talked about how God loves everyone in spite of who we are. And at the end of the service a young woman came up to me. She was struggling with her sexuality. She was broken in spirit. I'm sure she had experienced a good deal of rejection. She looked hopeless. I told her, "Jesus loves you! He wants to be your friend." She just fell into my arms. She was so broken that she could hardly stand. I desperately wanted her to know the depth of Jesus' love for her, just how much He wanted to be her friend. I think we need more compassion.

Compassion is entering into the pain of others. Jesus enters into our pains and griefs.

> What a Friend we have in Jesus,
>   All our sins and griefs to bear!
> What a privilege to carry
>   Everything to God in prayer!
> O what peace we often forfeit,
>   O what needless pain we bear,
> All because we do not carry
>   Everything to God in prayer![4]

## HIS CIRCLE OF FRIENDS

Jesus' life was marked by special friendships. To me that's so amazing. He was God in the flesh and He could have done anything He wanted to do. But He chose to invest in the lives of people. He chose twelve disciples and He made them His friends. And within that group of twelve were three who became His inner circle of friends: Peter, James, and John. They were with Him at crucial moments during His life. They were on the mountaintop with Him when He was transfigured and He talked to Moses and Elijah. They were with Him when He raised Jairus's daughter from the dead. And they were with Him in the garden of Gethsemane before He was taken to be crucified. At crucial moments, these three special friends were with Jesus.

And even within that inner circle of friends, there was one friend who was known as the "disciple whom Jesus loved" (John 13:23). This was John. He was the disciple who leaned his head on Jesus' breast at the Last Supper. I love that scene. John could smell His musk, touch His brow, hear His heartbeat, see the anguish on His face, taste His sorrow. With all five senses he came to know that Jesus was truly the God-man. He was Immanuel—God with us.

John was known as one of the Sons of Thunder. He met Jesus when he and his brother, James, were fishing on the Sea of Galilee. When Jesus called them to follow Him, they dropped their fishing nets immediately and followed after

> **As we enjoy God's friendship, our hearts are changed and we overflow in love to others.**

Him (see Matt. 4:18–22). John shows us what it means to walk through life with the love and friendship of Jesus as your constant companion. He developed a deep, abiding love for Jesus and wrote his letters to convince people who were saying that Jesus might not be the Son of God. He was overwhelmed by the love of God, as he exclaims in 1 John 3:1: "See what great love the Father has lavished on us, that we should be called children of God! And that is what we are! The reason the world does not know us is that it did not know him."

John was so captivated by his friendship with Jesus that he wrote his gospel to help everyone know that Jesus was the Son of God and that He gave His life to save sinners. He said that Jesus did so many things in the sight of His disciples that John couldn't write about all of them. But he wrote so that we might know that Jesus was this God manifested in the flesh, lived on earth, was crucified, risen, and went back to heaven. And He is now expecting His friends to carry out His mission to the world. His mission is for everyone to know that God loves them and wants to be their friend: "For God so loved the world that he gave his one and only Son, that whoever believes in him shall not perish but have eternal life" (John 3:16).

He continued that message of God's love in his three epistles, or letters, and said that everybody who is a friend of Jesus must love everyone else. We can't love God—who we've never seen—and claim to hate a person we see every day. He tied friendship and relationship with God to friendship and relationship with others. I love the Lord with all my heart; and I know He causes that love to overflow into the lives of other people. As we enjoy God's friendship, our hearts are changed and we overflow in love to others. He changes us. He reproduces His love in our hearts, and in the process we become loving people. Allowing that love to overflow has been my greatest joy.

## INTENTIONAL FRIEND

Jesus was intentional about becoming friends with His disciples. He spent time with them; for almost three years He walked through life with them. He shared His heart with them: "I no longer call you servants, because a servant does not know his master's business. Instead, I have called you friends, for everything that I learned from my Father I have made known to you" (John 15:15). He taught them at every opportunity. They saw Him weep at the tomb of His friend Lazarus. He made Himself vulnerable to them, which is an act of humility.[5] His example helps connect us with people because it demonstrates that we are not very different from one another at all. What a model of true friendship for us!

Young folks today talk about "ride or die" friends. That's somebody who will be with you no matter what happens in life. Back in my day this was called a "blood brother." There's a crucial lesson about friendship in this. Everybody needs good friends to do life with; but in a pinch you need a ride or die brother or sister. Jesus had that in this inner circle of men, and especially with John. If Jesus, the God-man, who was all-powerful and knew all things, needed friends and wanted friends, I think all of us need friends in our lives. I think there's a deep yearning in all our hearts for true, meaningful friendships.

One of those special friendships for me came about in an unusual way. When former Governor Barbour was running for office in Mississippi, he invited a group of black pastors to meet with him at a restaurant and talk. The group at first said, "No! He's a Republican!" I said, "Look here, he is going to win the election anyway. Why don't we go over and talk to him and bring him our big issues? Let's be tough on him." They listened to me, and when the meeting got started I asked him, "What kind of governor are you going to be?" After he was elected, he thought that my helping him was key to his victory and he recognized me. We became very good friends after that.

## MEN NEED FRIENDSHIP

It can be hard for men to develop friendships. We have become captive to the American idea of individualism and competition. It's easy to see other people as our competitors rather than someone we might actually need. But we do need each other. When I think of Jesus and His circle of friends, I think that's what we yearn for. That's what we desperately need. Growing up without a mother, without a father, and then losing my brother left me at a deficit of love and friendship. That kind of deficit can be painful. But God blessed me with such special friends. Most of my friends did not have a brother, or if they had a brother, there was some deficiency in their relationship. I have become the brother they needed; they have become the brothers I needed.[6] And these friendships have sustained me and have filled the friendship void in my heart.

## THE GOD-MAN WHO DIED FOR US

Jesus came to show us how to live and to model true friendship. And He came to make the ultimate sacrifice. He came into the world to save us from our sins. While Adam, Abraham, Moses, and David came up short, He lived a perfect life without sin. So He was qualified to die to pay for our sin. He was qualified to serve as the sacrificial Lamb as well as the scapegoat.

John defined the greatest form of love as dying for a friend: "Greater love has no one than this: to lay down one's life for one's friends" (John 15:13). That is surely the ultimate friend. And it's the ultimate test of friendship. As Jesus was dying on the cross for our sins, it was His most beloved friend, John, who stood at the foot of the cross. All the other disciples had deserted Him. They had run in fear of losing their own lives. But John remained to the very end. And in His dying breaths Jesus commended His mother to John, the disciple He loved. He had at least two brothers, James and Jude, who it would have been assumed would care for their mother. The writer of Proverbs said, "One who has unreliable friends soon comes to ruin, but there is a friend who sticks closer than a brother" (18:24). John was like that. He was the friend who stuck closer than a brother. He would take care of Mary, the mother of Jesus, for the rest of her life. That's a picture of true friendship. I'm so grateful that, like John, I have a friend in Jesus.

In *Peace Child,* Don Richardson shares the story of how the Sawi people of Irian Jaya came to understand that they could be saved through Jesus Christ. For a long time, he and his family tried to find a way to communicate the gospel to this tribe. Their prayers were finally answered. They learned that the Sawi only understood one demonstration of kindness. If a father gave his own son to his enemy, his sacrificial deed showed that he could be trusted. And everyone who touched that child was brought into a friendly relationship with the father. The Sawi were then taught that in a similar way God's beloved Son could bring them eternal peace.[7]

God did that for every one of us. He gave us His Son, Jesus. And Jesus gave His life to pay the penalty for sin. It cost Him something to be my friend. When I watched *The Passion of the Christ*, directed by Mel Gibson, I was undone as I watched Jesus struggle up the hill called Calvary with the cross weighing Him down. I was undone when the Romans took strings of leather with sharp rocks tied into them and beat Him mercilessly. Yet the cry of my heart was, *He can take it! He can take it! He's got to take it! We need a Savior!* He died a gruesome death to pay for all my sins. And just as the Old Testament Scriptures had foretold, He rose from the grave three days later. He was truly the Son of God. He was fully man and fully God. He alone was able to once and for all fix what was broken in the garden of Eden . . . and to become a friend who is like none other.

> There's not a Friend like the lowly Jesus:
>    No, not one! no, not one!
> None else could heal all our souls' diseases:
>    No, not one! no, not one!
>
>    Jesus knows all about our struggles;
>       He will guide 'til the day is done:
>    There's not a Friend like the lowly Jesus:
>       No, not one! no, not one![8]

"Why do you eat and drink with
tax collectors and sinners?"

———————

Luke 5:30

# CHAPTER 5

# Friend of Prostitutes, Thieves, and the Outsider

*Josephine Butler was a well-bred, middle-class Victorian wife and mother. The year was 1828 and women were expected to take care of the home and children. The tragic loss of her daughter caused her to "plunge into the heart of some human misery, and to say . . . to afflicted people, 'I understand. I, too, have suffered.'" That path led her to love and serve women who were considered scum and subhuman: prostitutes. She responded to them with compassion and treated them with respect. She invited many of them to live with her; she began opening small hospitals for prostitutes who were seriously ill, and homes to house them while they learned work skills. She was able to stand firm against a roar of opposition because her actions were rooted deeply in her faith in Christ and the redemptive worth He offered every person.[1]*

No one would have expected Josephine Butler to get her hands dirty serving people who were social outcasts. She was expected to be like most of the other women of her time. She was to take care of her children and maintain a good home. Surely it was beneath her station in life to be friends with people who ran afoul of the law and decency . . . people like prostitutes.

I can only imagine the expectation of the people of Israel as they awaited the coming of the Messiah. God had not spoken through a prophet for four hundred years, and many of them were looking for a prophet to point the way. Others longed for the glory days when David was king and Israel was the greatest power in the Near East. How would He come? What would He be like? Would He come into royal lineage? Would He come as a ruling king, riding on a stallion? Would He finally put the Romans in their place and liberate His people and the nation of Israel? Would He put His people into positions of power?

## HUMBLE BEGINNINGS

His humble beginnings on earth were a huge window into the kinds of friends He would seek. And so was His lineage. Tucked into His family line on the human side are some powerful witnesses to what matters most to the heart of God. Tamar is there. She deceived her father-in-law by dressing up like a prostitute so she could have his child after he reneged on a family duty to her. Rahab is there. She was the prostitute who helped the Israelites take the city of Jericho. Ruth is there. She was an outsider, a pagan Gentile. And Bathsheba is there, the woman who bore David's sin.

All of these were women who were at the mercy of a culture that did not value them. Their culture told them that they were less than other folks. Yet God intervened in each of their lives to affirm their dignity. One of our greatest problems today is that we curse people instead of affirming their worth. We think that it's up to us to decide who has dignity and who doesn't. But it's not up to us to give anybody dignity. God already did that. He created every person in His own image—the *Imago Dei*. He created mankind so that we might know Him and make Him known, serve Him, and worship Him forever. So every person already has that God-given worth. It's our responsibility and privilege to affirm it in others.

We affirm individuals by how we greet and respond to them, by how we look them in the eyes and acknowledge their presence. An African proverb says, "When I saw you from afar, I thought you were a monster. When you got closer, I thought you were just an animal. When you got even closer, I saw that you were a human, but when we were face to face I realized that you were my brother." I believe this is true in so many ways. We observe people from a distance and make judgments about them that convince us to keep them at a distance. Tolerance is the space between when we first meet a person and when we decide that we don't like them. We've erased this space. We need to make space to get to know people. Oh, how I wish that we could get close enough to one another to realize that we can be friends, that we *are* brothers and sisters.

## FRIEND OF BROKEN WOMEN

Jesus showed us how to cross all the spoken and unspoken boundary lines when He met a Samaritan woman at a well. She was an outcast. We know that because the respected women of the city came to draw water in the cool of the day. But this woman came alone, in the heat of the day when the sun was at its highest

HE CALLS ME FRIEND

> No matter what I do, when I'm finished with my doing, I am met by His grace, His love, and His eternal friendship.

point, because she wanted to avoid others, and their looks of judgment and disgust. But this day would change her life forever. The Hound of Heaven was about to capture another precious soul.

Jesus met this despised woman. The story is told in John 4. Social norms dictated He was not supposed to speak to a woman in private. That went against all of their laws and customs. But Jesus greeted her. He treated her with respect. He wanted to make her His friend. The offer of friendship is an affirmation of dignity. Jesus put her first in every way. He was needy, thirsty; He demonstrated humility by making Himself vulnerable. He could have condemned her for her lifestyle and made her feel unworthy. He could have called her what most Jews did when they spoke of Samaritans: "unclean." Instead He said, "Will you give me a drink?" Those words must have startled her. She couldn't have expected Him to actually speak to her. She was used to men turning their eyes away when she approached, at least the kind of man you take home to meet your father. She reacted by saying, "You're a Jew, I'm a Samaritan. We have nothing to do with one another."

And though everything she said was true, Jesus' love broke through. He drank from her cup as a sign of true fellowship. He took the time to talk with her and answer her questions. His actions toward her demonstrated respect and honor and love. Love is the essence of God. Jesus showed us that nothing is more important than love.

If I speak in the tongues of men or of angels, but do not have love, I am only a resounding gong or a clanging cymbal. If I have the gift of prophecy and can fathom all mysteries and all knowledge, and if I have a faith that can move mountains, but do not have love, I am nothing. If I give all I possess to the poor and give over my body to hardship that I may boast, but do not have love, I gain nothing. . . .

And now these three remain: faith, hope and love. But the greatest of these is love. —1 Corinthians 13:1–3, 13

Yes, the greatest of these is love. The love of God is revealed through His grace. And grace is bigger than all our sins. I am grateful above all for this truth. God's love and grace will always outrun my sin. No matter what I do, when I'm finished with my doing, I am met by His grace, His love, and His eternal friendship.

Jesus demonstrated the depths of God's grace. His love and friendship for this marginalized woman transformed her life. She had come to the well dejected, sad, and lonely. She left excited and determined to tell everybody in Samaria that she had found a friend in Jesus and would never be alone again.

This Samaritan woman was not the only social outcast Jesus befriended. Again and again we read in Scripture about how He went outside the expected lines to call friends to Himself. Matthew was another one of those unexpected friends.

## FRIEND OF DESPISED MEN

In *Leadership Revolution*, I observed that "it's important to recognize that Jesus did not find His followers at leadership conferences or in the halls of academia. He didn't check to see whether or not they had seminary degrees or how well they had done on their standardized tests. He didn't even ask for references. He didn't put out the word far and wide that He was looking for people. Instead, He just looked around and decided to work with those who were nearby."[2] One of those who was blessed to be nearby was a tax collector named Matthew.

In Jesus' day there were chief tax collectors and tax collectors. Chief tax collectors contracted with the Roman Empire to collect the taxes that were due. They were notorious for adding on high fees and taking advantage of their people. They hired people like Matthew to sit at tollbooths to collect the taxes on just about everything: all goods, merchandise, and services. Every vendor, including the prostitutes, paid taxes on their business. Matthew was a tax collector.

As Jesus walked through Capernaum, He set His eyes on Matthew at the tax collector's booth. He said to him, "Follow me," and immediately Matthew got up from the booth and followed after Jesus. I am struck by Matthew's instant response. He must have sensed that Jesus was going to fulfill his longing for friendship and meaning. He was despised because he exploited his own people. He was seen as the worst of sinners in Jewish culture. When the Jews cursed someone, about the worst thing they could call them was "tax collector."

When Matthew hosted a dinner at his house with other tax collectors and those called sinners, Jesus was the guest of honor. Jesus had chosen to befriend this outcast the good religious folks hated. And they were up in arms that Jesus would do this. His response to them was, "It is not the healthy who need a doctor, but the sick. I have not come to call the righteous, but sinners to repentance" (Luke 5:31–32). This had to be shocking and wonderful news to Matthew and his guests! Jesus wanted them!

Jesus was going to upset the religious elite once again when He called another tax collector. Zacchaeus was a chief tax collector. He was filthy rich from his schemes and plots to take from his own people. But one day while passing through Jericho, Jesus saw Zacchaeus. He called him to Himself and went to eat at his house. Zacchaeus, with joy, received Jesus as friend and vowed to give half of his possessions to the poor and to repay four times anything he had cheated another person out of.

Zacchaeus and Matthew, both tax collectors, accepted Jesus' offer of friendship and love. Matthew would become one of the twelve disciples and would write one of the Gospels. This former tax collector who took advantage of his people in order to make money would be used by God to convince those very people that Jesus was truly the Son of God. God used him to record the words of the Sermon on the Mount, in which Jesus set forth the demands of kingdom living. From the moment that Matthew got up from his tollbooth, he never looked back. I suppose he was so very grateful that Jesus didn't see him as an outcast. Jesus saw him as a friend, and as someone who was useful for kingdom work.

## FRIEND OF THE OUTCAST

Friend of prostitutes? Yes! Friend of despised tax collectors? Yes! But Jesus was going to confound their religious rules by reaching to the very lowest level of society. If there was anything like a caste system in Jesus' day, I suppose at the lowest level we would find the lepers. Lepers were seen as unclean and were forced to live outside of the city limits. They were not allowed to worship in the temple. If they were walking down the street and someone approached them, they were required to shout, "Unclean! Unclean!" to alert the person to not come close. They lived in leper colonies with other lepers. Leprosy was almost the sentence of death; surely Jesus would not go there. Surely the Son of God, the God-man, would not risk becoming unclean by touching one of these outcasts!

> I know what it feels like to be at the low end of the totem pole. I know what it feels like when "good" people look down their noses at you. Something on the inside dies over and over again.

One day while traveling along the border of Galilee toward Jerusalem, ten lepers saw Jesus (Luke 17:11–19). They stood at a distance away from Him and shouted, "Jesus, Master, have pity on us!" He was moved with compassion and told them to go and show themselves to the priest. The priest would be able to confirm that they were no longer unclean, that they had been healed. As soon as they began walking to find the priest, they were all healed. One of them returned and fell at Jesus' feet, thanking Him for the healing.

And Matthew shares his own story of Jesus healing a leper. Only this time it would be different. With the ten lepers Jesus simply spoke to them from a distance and told them to see the priest. This time He would actually use physical touch to heal the leper. When Jesus came down from the mountain after preaching the Sermon on the Mount, many people flocked after Him. A leper approached Him and said, "Lord, if you are willing, you can make me clean." Jesus was not repulsed by the man. He was not concerned with the Law that required no physical contact with a leper. Instead of turning away, Jesus reached out His hand and touched the man. He said, "I am willing. Be clean" (Matt. 8:2–3). And in that very instant this leper was completely cured of his leprosy. He had been touched by the hand of Jesus! As with the other lepers, Jesus told him to go show himself to the priest to confirm that he was now free of the dreaded disease.

I can only imagine the joy that must have filled the heart of that man. Probably for years he had been forced to watch life pass him by. He was an outsider . . . outside all social circles . . . outside . . . alone . . . rejected. He was like so many of the forgotten people of our day who have slipped through the cracks. They're outsiders. They're at the bottom rung of society and they are alone, desperately in need of someone who will be like Jesus for them and will heal them with the offer of friendship and love. I know what it feels like to be at the low end of the totem pole. I know what it feels like when "good" people look down their noses at you. Something on the inside dies over and over again.

## HE ENFOLDS THE OUTSIDER

I love it that Jesus comes after those kinds of folks. The Hound of Heaven makes room for the rejected, the thrown-away masses. And I guess the real question is, *If God Himself loves and wants the outcasts, why don't we?* Why do we walk away rather than walk toward them? Why do we refuse to look them in the eyes and feel their pain? The stories of people like Mother Teresa and Josephine Butler—and many others we don't hear about—are amazing. But their actions shouldn't be the exception: their stories should be the story of everyone who has been saved and who is a friend of Jesus. Tim Keller posted this statement on Twitter recently: "Bible-believing religious people often miss the gospel. Just because you believe in the Bible doesn't mean you understand it. Over and over the tax collectors, prostitutes, and the amoral come to Jesus, while the religious miss who He is."[3]

The outcasts come to Jesus because they are drawn by His love, His grace, His heart for them. My heart aches for the church to see that this is our call today. To love them in! To draw them with love and grace, the same love that we received when we claimed Jesus as our Savior. It still works!

We can learn a lot about true friendship from Jesus. He wasn't put off by sin. No amount of sin kept Him from being friends with someone. He seemed to be drawn to people who were outsiders and outcasts—the truly hurting folks. His love and friendship were so powerful that broken hearts and broken lives were healed. I think we miss out on rich opportunities for friendship so often because we judge people on the outside. We are put off because they don't look like us or because they don't fit a certain mold. I'm grateful for special friends who were able to get past their first impressions of me and become true friends. They were models of tolerance. They made space between when they first met me and when they made a decision about whether they'd like me or not. I'll let Randy and Joan share the story of our friendship in their own words.

Let's Hear It from Randy and Joan Nabors:

# *Friendship*
# IS TOLERANT

My wife, Joan, remembers the first time we met John Perkins. It was in 1975 at the National Conference on Race and Reconciliation held in Atlanta, Georgia. We were put in a small group, and Joan says that as we sat down, she noticed this black man sitting there, seemingly off to the back. He wasn't dressed very sharp, and at first appearance didn't seem like he was going to be the most intellectual or strategic thinker in the room. If I remember correctly, in that small group was C. Peter Wagner of Fuller Seminary, David Mains, and Clarence Hilliard of Circle Church in Chicago, Joan and I, and John Perkins. By 1975, Joan and I had been married for four years and I, Randy, was a student at Covenant Theological Seminary. Joan and I were the youngest people in the group.

It was a surprise when John began to speak. At first there was nothing to hint at why he should have been in the group or in the discussion. He wasn't an academic; he didn't seem to hold a powerful position in evangelical Christianity. He was an unimposing black man. He wasn't smooth, but his face looked like he had done some living. He looked and acted "country" from Mississippi and sounded like it. Actually, he looked like he just came from working on the farm. He seemed entirely too humble and out of place to be much of a factor in our future, let alone the future of the church in the United States. John had the habit of using his hands to wipe off his lips as he spoke and he wasn't doing anything to impress people or compete for our attention. Everything about him just set us up for a great surprise.

Joan is African American and I am white. John has told us over the years that our marriage means a lot to him. It has signified, along with the raising of our family and the pastoring of a cross-cultural church, our commitment to racial reconciliation. He tells us we have been a testimony and an example of much of what he has been fighting for during his life. I am sure he didn't think this initially about us, and I am sure he had many questions about who we were and what we were about when he first saw us. Even those of us intensely committed to reconciliation often have a first-look bias that we have to plow through to have an honest relationship; people can and do surprise us.

One of the great and wonderful blessings of our lives has been a friendship with John Perkins. Beginning from that first meeting he has taught us so much about community economic development. Just the idea that Christians could do something in the name of Jesus to impact the conditions of poor people was a revelation to us. We had grown up in one of the housing projects of Newark, New Jersey. Joan and I were native to urban poverty and its environment. We were extremely conscious of racism, poverty, crime, violence, and the seeming absence of most of the evangelical church in dealing with these issues. We understood and practiced evangelism, as John had when he first came back to Mississippi to do children's evangelism in the schools. Our home church in Newark was a champion of urban, cross-cultural evangelism. They were a congregation that extended mercy to people and helped in various ways. They brought food to my house when my family had none, and they taught me how to do the same while I was a teenager in the youth group.

John opened our eyes to opportunities for meaningful impact in poor communities. Not only did John's comments and questions in that group reveal to us that this man understood the issues but that he had lived them. We would later find out how much he had suffered on his way to a commitment to reconciliation. His godliness, humility, and dead-on prophetic voice about and against the injustice fostered by racism (with his amazing and honest biblical and societal insights) just captivated us.

We were amazed that a man who had so many reasons to hate and be suspicious of white people could be so kind. Joan and I had grown up in a context of black radicalism—with people we had known and grown up with becoming black Muslims, some in the Black Panthers—and experienced the Newark riots of 1967 and in 1968 after the assassination of Dr. Martin Luther King Jr. Racial hostility was becoming an almost normal environment for us to navigate as an interracial couple. None of the people we knew, and who were so angry, had ever suffered as much as John Perkins. We just had the impression that if we had ever met a man who had been with Jesus it was John. The Bible just seemed to be dripping from this man.

One of the delights of our heart is to have our daughter love and admire John Perkins. Keren was a student at Reformed Theological Seminary in Jackson. She began to attend John's Bible study at 5:30 in the morning once a week. We couldn't believe our daughter could get up that early in the morning, so it impressed us, and it impressed John. John even came as "Honorary Grandfather" to her wedding when Keren married her husband, Alex. Coach Wayne Gordon has said John makes everyone feel like he is their special friend, and it is true, that is one of his gifts and great personal skills. We are humbled that he has loved and befriended us, made us feel important to the kingdom, constantly encouraged us, and included us in his fellowship whenever we have seen him. I wish we all knew how to be a friend like that.

Randy and Joan Nabors

*Randy is the urban and mercy coordinator for Mission to North America with New City Network. Randy and Joan make their home in Chattanooga, TN.*

# Part Three

# FRIENDSHIP WITH THE HOLY SPIRIT

"*You have searched me, LORD,*
*and you know me.*"

———————

Psalm 139:1

# CHAPTER 6

# The God Who Dwells Within

*There is a story about a twelve-year-old boy who got saved and became a friend of Jesus at a revival. Later that day, his friends started questioning him about it. One said, "Did you see a vision?" Another said, "Did you hear God speak?" The boy answered all of these questions with a simple, "No." "Well, how did you know you were saved?" they asked. The boy replied, "It's like when you catch a fish, you can't see the fish or hear the fish; you just feel him tugging on your line: I just felt God tugging on my heart."[1]*

For more than sixty years I've been just like that little boy who was saved at that revival. For these many years I've felt God tugging on my heart telling me which way to turn, telling me what to do, reminding me of His promises. It was God the Holy Spirit who planted the restlessness in my heart after visiting the prison in California and seeing all those black boys who were just like me. I went back home to my good life, but He would not let me forget what I had seen. He would not let me forget their faces. I felt like David must have felt when he said, "Where can I go from your Spirit? Where can I flee from your presence?

If I go up to the heavens, you are there; if I make my bed in the depths, you are there" (Ps. 139:7–8). The Hound of Heaven who relentlessly pursued me to become my friend continued His pursuit to make sure I did what He wanted me to do. That's how the Holy Spirit works in my life. He is my closest friend.

The Holy Spirit is the awesome presence of God. He is what the old preacher called omnipresent. That means that He is everywhere at the same time. God the Son came to tabernacle with us, to live among us, and to allow us to touch Him and know that He was God. But before He went back to heaven He promised His disciples that He would send another Comforter who would be with them always. That Comforter is the Holy Spirit and He comes to live in us. To know Him is to know that He's ever with us.

## HE IS A PERSON

The Holy Spirit is the third person of the Trinity. Millard J. Erickson's *Christian Theology* helps us know why it's important for us to know who God the Holy Spirit is: "The Spirit is important, since he provides contact between the believer and God." He goes on to share that because we live in a time that stresses the experiential, it's through the work of the Holy Spirit that we feel the presence of God within us.[2] The Holy Spirit is the power and the presence of God living in the hearts of believers.

> The Holy Spirit uses circumstances in our lives to cause us to cry out to God and to seek His will and His purposes.

102

Growing up as I did in Mississippi, I didn't have much interaction with church folk. So my understanding of the Holy Spirit was limited to what I knew of Pentecostals. I thought that the Holy Spirit just made folks get happy and speak in tongues. I didn't realize that He was a person; that He was God. And even after walking with the Lord for these many years, it can still be confusing and hard to put into words exactly who the Holy Spirit is. But I know that He is supernatural. He is the very presence of God. When Jesus talked to the Samaritan woman, He told her that God is a Spirit and that He must be worshiped in spirit and in truth.

I have come to know Him as the true Friend who sticks closer than a brother. "He walks with me and He talks with me, and He tells me that I am His own" as the words of that beloved hymn "In the Garden" express this truth. I don't know where I would be today if He had not done the hard work of chiseling through bad habits and smoothing out rough places in my heart. And He continues to do that work.

We can't know God apart from the Spirit. He gives us a hunger and a thirst for God and for the things of God. It's been said that "when you desire God as truly as you desired to breathe the air you just breathed—then you shall find God."[3]

I don't think it's in our fleshly will to know God like that. But the Holy Spirit uses circumstances in our lives to cause us to cry out to God and to seek His will and His purposes. He makes us desperate for God's will in our lives. It was from the desperation in a jail cell in Brandon, Mississippi, that the Holy Spirit drew me to God's purposes for my life. Lying there after being beaten by the police, I was full of venom and anger. (This story has been told in other places, but briefly, this incident occurred during the struggle for civil rights.[4]) I wanted to strike back. I wanted to do some damage. But out of that agony and suffering He pointed me to a better way. He showed me a higher road that would lead to true joy and peace. That was what my heart longed for. There was only one way to get it. And it required me to loosen my hold on anger and bitterness and allow Him to show me the way out.

## HE COMES WITH POWER

The Holy Spirit is constantly working to make God known to us, and I believe that He usually makes Himself known through one of our senses so that the memory will be marked forever. And that's what He did at Pentecost. Those who were there would never forget the fire that looked like tongues that rested on each person as they spoke God's message.

When God the Son came to earth in physical form He came as a baby, born to a virgin, in a quiet village called Bethlehem. But when God the Holy Spirit came, He rushed on the scene causing an uproar that got everybody's attention. The gospel writer Luke described it this way:

> When the day of Pentecost came, they were all together in one place. Suddenly a sound like the blowing of a violent wind came from heaven and filled the whole house where they were sitting. They saw what seemed to be tongues of fire that separated and came to rest on each of them. All of them were filled with the Holy Spirit and began to speak in other tongues as the Spirit enabled them.
>
> Now there were staying in Jerusalem God-fearing Jews from every nation under heaven. When they heard this sound, a crowd came together in bewilderment, because each one heard their own language being spoken. Utterly amazed, they asked: "Aren't all these who

are speaking Galileans? Then how is it that each of us hears them in our native language? Parthians, Medes and Elamites; residents of Mesopotamia, Judea and Cappadocia, Pontus and Asia, Phrygia and Pamphylia, Egypt and the parts of Libya near Cyrene; visitors from Rome (both Jews and converts to Judaism); Cretans and Arabs—we hear them declaring the wonders of God in our own tongues!" Amazed and perplexed, they asked one another, "What does this mean?"—Acts 2:1–12

When this new Comforter, the Holy Spirit, came, His presence literally filled the place. There were the eleven disciples along with more than one hundred of Jesus' followers. The Holy Spirit filled them with His presence. What appeared to be tongues of fire rested on each of them, and they spoke in languages that were not natural to them. Everyone was able to hear the gospel in their own language or dialect. The Jewish people spoke Aramaic. They saw the Gentile languages as "uncultured and guttural."[5] But in this miraculous event God opened the mouths of these Jewish believers, and they found themselves speaking in words that reached those present, including those who had been seen as outsiders. The Holy Spirit allowed every person in the crowd, Jews and Gentiles, to hear God's invitation to be His friend in their own language! As we will soon see with Cornelius and his family, God was widening the net to include all people, of all ethnicities, from all over the world. And the Holy Spirit made it so that if someone was from Greece and spoke Greek, they heard God's invitation to friendship in Greek. Whatever language someone spoke, they heard the gospel message in their own language.

The apostle Peter explained that what was happening was the fulfillment of an Old Testament prophecy. The prophet

Joel said that God would "pour out [His] Spirit on all people," and this was the fulfillment of that prophesy (Joel 2:28–32). And then Peter shared with them the gospel, that Jesus was the Messiah and that He had died for their sins. After Peter finished preaching, more than three thousand people became friends of Jesus. The Holy Spirit accomplished what He had set out to do. He had made God known to them and many of them became His friends.

## HE RECONCILES PEOPLE

God repeated that same awesome experience again when He told Peter to visit Cornelius, a Roman centurion. He was not a Jew. But God was getting ready to do a new thing. Once again, God through the Holy Spirit would show that the special relationship God offers is for everyone, not only with the Jews. God loves all people and His desire is that no man or woman be left outside of His love. Cornelius and his entire household were overwhelmed by God's offer of friendship and fellowship. They were baptized right away. (You can read this exciting story in Acts 10!) The Holy Spirit makes God known. But He doesn't just make God known to us as individuals. He doesn't just reconcile people to God. He reconciles us with each other. The Holy Spirit drew the Gentile Cornelius and his family into reconciled relationship with God and also with Peter, who was a Jew. This was reconciliation on display in the early church. And let me tell you, whatever the divisions we have between people and groups today, they had it just as much back then. A devout Jew just didn't go into the home of a Gentile or enjoy a meal with a Gentile; and the Jews who were waiting for the Messiah didn't dream that the message of the gospel was for anyone other than Jews. It took the work of the Holy Spirit to work out reconciliation between Jews and Gentiles. And the Holy Spirit is working to do the same thing today, to bring reconciliation to groups and people who have been in opposing camps. He works to bring His friends together across every line that separates us.

## HE GIVES BOLDNESS TO HIS FRIENDS

After the Holy Spirit came at Pentecost, the very next mention of the Holy Spirit in Scripture is when Peter and John had been arrested and jailed overnight for healing a lame man.

> Then Peter, filled with the Holy Spirit, said to them: "Rulers and elders of the people! If we are being called to account today for an act of kindness shown to a man who was lame and are being asked how he was healed, then know this, you and all the people of Israel: It is by the name of Jesus Christ of Nazareth, whom you cruci-fied but whom God raised from the dead, that this man stands before you healed. Jesus is 'the stone you builders rejected, which has become the cornerstone.' Salvation is found in no one else, for there is no other name under heaven given to mankind by which we must be saved."
> —Acts 4:8–12

Peter was filled with the Holy Spirit and was not afraid to speak boldly for Christ even though he could have been put back in prison, beaten, and punished severely. When people saw the courage of Peter and John and realized that they were unedu-cated, ordinary men, they were amazed. And they realized that being friends with Jesus is what gave them this kind of boldness.

Like Peter and John, I don't have a lot of formal education. I am just an ordinary man. My English is not very eloquent, and I'm usually surrounded by people who are pretty educated. It can be discouraging to look at the faces of these people and feel like you have to prove yourself time and time again. But my friend the Holy Spirit gives me the boldness to stand and to speak. And He always fills my mouth with His Word. The Holy Spirit is softening hearts to hear the message of reconciliation to God and to one another whether rich, poor, educated, or uneducated.

It's beginning to look like giving us boldness to share the Word and talk about Jesus is one of the Holy Spirit's main jobs. In Acts 4:31, after Paul and John were released, the believers got together and prayed. After they prayed, they were "all filled with the Holy Spirit and spoke the word of God boldly." And then in Acts 6, Stephen was described as a "man full of faith and of the Holy Spirit" (v. 5). We see Stephen's boldness on display after he was arrested for preaching the gospel. He stood and boldly challenged those who had crucified Jesus. Even as they prepared to stone him to death, "Stephen, full of the Holy Spirit, looked up to heaven and saw the glory of God, and Jesus standing at the right hand of God. 'Look,' he said, 'I see heaven open and the Son of Man standing at the right hand of God'" (Acts 7:55–56).

> **That's uncommon boldness. To be able to stand in front of folks who are going to kill you for your faith and be able to fix your eyes on heaven and find peace. That's the kind of boldness we desperately need today.**

That's uncommon boldness. To be able to stand in front of folks who are going to kill you for your faith and be able to fix your eyes on heaven and find peace. I think this must be the kind of boldness that many of the martyrs had. It was the power of the Holy Spirit within them. I'm sure that it's what Polycarp had. The account of Polycarp's martyrdom is one of the earliest written about apart from the New Testament. When the soldiers came to arrest him, his friends tried to get him to run for his life. He refused. "Soldiers then grabbed him to nail him to a stake, but Polycarp stopped them: 'Leave me as I am. For He who grants me to endure the fire will enable me also to remain on the pyre unmoved, without the security you desire from nails.' He prayed aloud, the fire was lit, and his flesh was consumed. The chronicler of this martyrdom said it was 'not as burning flesh but as bread baking or as gold and silver refined in a furnace.'"[6]

That's the kind of boldness we desperately need today. In a day and time when people are trying with all their might to fill the friendship void in their lives with money, possessions, and power, we need to be bold enough to tell them the truth. Friendship with God is the only thing that will fill that empty place. We don't need to be afraid to reach out to people, to become friends, and to tell them about Jesus. The Holy Spirit gives us the same boldness that He gave to Peter and John and Stephen and Polycarp. We have it—but we don't use it. It's like having an unlimited resource that we have never used. It's like having a million dollars in the bank and living in a homeless shelter because you don't know you have that much money available. I want to be bold enough to speak up for Him every chance I get.

## HE IS EVEN MORE THAN ALL THAT

The truth of the matter is that the Holy Spirit does a whole lot more in our lives than make us bold. He's a teacher. He convicts us of sin. He guides us in His way. He produces fruit in our lives that equips us to be friends with everybody. We'll talk about all of that in the next chapter. But for right now, I hope we can wrestle with this truth: the Holy Spirit came to make God known, to make us friends with God, and to give us boldness to share the good news with people who desperately need good news. When I think about the scores of people who can be set free with this good news, it becomes overwhelming. I don't want anybody that I know to miss out on having Him as a friend. The world desperately needs this Friend who lives within and fills the empty place.

One of my favorite songs celebrates the truth that once you become a friend of God, a friend of Jesus, a friend of the Holy Spirit . . . you are never, ever alone. This is wonderful news for a world full of lonely people!

> I've seen the lightning flashing,
>   And heard the thunder roll;
> I've felt sin's breakers dashing,
>   Trying to conquer my soul;
> I've heard the voice of Jesus,
>   Telling me still to fight on;
> He promised never to leave me,
>   Never to leave me alone.

No, never alone,
  No, never alone,
He promised never to leave me,
  Never to leave me alone.[7]

The Holy Spirit is God with you, God within your heart, every moment of every day. You cannot be lonely when He is your ever-present friend. We can rejoice in this eternal truth!

"The fruit of the Spirit is not push, drive, climb, grasp, and trample. Life is more than a climb to the top of the heap."

———

Richard J. Foster

# CHAPTER 7

# The Fruit of Friendship

*Ben Hooper was born on October 13, 1870 in Tennessee. Life was hard for him. He suffered the taunts of children at school because he did not have a father and would hide at recess and lunchtime. He avoided going to stores for fear of hearing, "Who's your daddy?" When he was twelve years old he went to church but would always arrive late and leave early to avoid people. But one Sunday a new minister came to their church and gave the benediction before Ben could escape. As he tried to slip out of the sanctuary he felt a big hand grab his shoulder. And he heard the repeated question again, "Who are you, son? Whose boy are you?" Ben felt the old weight come on him.* Even the preacher is putting me down. *But he looked up and saw the preacher smiling as he said, "Wait a minute! I know who you are. I see the family resemblance now. You are a child of God!" With that he patted the boy on his shoulder and said, "Boy, you've got a great inheritance. Go and claim it." Ben smiled for the first time in a long time and walked out the door a changed person. He later said that was the greatest single sentence anyone had ever said to him. He would become the governor of Tennessee years later.*[1]

As many as 25 percent of children in America are like Ben. They're being raised in homes without a father.[2] There's an epidemic of fatherlessness in our country. But my joy is that if we are friends of God, we have a Father. Just like Ben, if we are friends of God, we can say and know that we are children of God. We have a great inheritance to go and claim. Galatians 4:6 tells us, "Because you are his sons, God sent the Spirit of his Son into our hearts, the Spirit who calls out, 'Abba, Father.'"

We are part of God's family. He is our heavenly Father, and we should all see the family resemblance. The work of the Holy Spirit in the life of a believer is to make us look like Jesus. He is our teacher. He is our guide. He is our Comforter. He lives within us every moment of every day to produce the character of Christ in our lives.

In *The Deeper Life*, Daniel Henderson says, "If I wanted my children to understand some truths in life, I would likely do three things: try to explain these truths, endeavor to demonstrate them, and even hire a personal tutor to assure that they are really learning these realities. God, in His perfection, has provided a personal indwelling tutor. The Holy Spirit is the very presence of God, illumining our minds and guiding our hearts to a transformational understanding and application of who He is."[3]

The problem for every one of us is sin. There's a war going on between our flesh and our spirit. Before we became friends with God we were ruled by our flesh. We did what we wanted to do. Our flesh is easily tempted to do what is wrong. I remember a time when I sinned and I was almost madly desiring that thing. We can become possessed by our own will. But now that we are friends of God, the Holy Spirit also lives within. We have two spirits alive within, and as friends of God, our prayer must always be, "Father, thy will be done on earth as it is in heaven. . . . Lead me not into temptation, but deliver me from evil." I need for that to be my prayer each and every day.

This Cherokee fable helps us understand what happens when we become a friend of Jesus:

> Once, an old man and his grandson were walking through the woods when the grandfather turned to the young man and said, "Young one, inside all of us there is a battle raging between two wolves. You have felt it even in your young years, and I have felt it all my life. One of the wolves is evil—he is anger, envy, greed, regret, arrogance, resentment, lies, hatred, and ego. The other is good—he is love, joy, peace, hope, humility, kindness, empathy, generosity, compassion, truth and faith. Everyone has this battle going on inside them."
>
> They walked a little further in silence, until the young boy stopped and asked, "Grandfather, which wolf will win?"
>
> The wise, old man simply replied, "The one you feed."[4]

The old man was right. We can feed the evil wolf of the flesh, and if we do, we will not live the life that God is calling us to. But if we feed the good wolf, by obeying the Holy Spirit, we will win the battle. And it's an everyday battle. Every day we have to decide to engage that battle.

The fruit that the flesh produces is ugly and destroys our ability to be friends with God and with others:

> The acts of the flesh are obvious: sexual immorality, impurity and debauchery; idolatry and witchcraft; hatred, discord, jealousy, fits of rage, selfish ambition, dissensions, factions and envy; drunkenness, orgies, and the like. I warn you, as I did before, that those who live like this will not inherit the kingdom of God. —Galatians 5:19–21

But I thank God for what the Holy Spirit is doing in our lives. As we begin to cooperate with the Holy Spirit and follow His leading, we are being made over to be like Jesus. And we are excited about being friends with others, regardless of their color or station in life, just as Jesus was. The Holy Spirit begins producing fruit in our lives that is evidence that we belong to Him. And the fruit that He produces is always focused on us reaching out to others, loving them, and helping them become friends of Jesus.

> As much as we want to do good, sometimes we fail. But I always remember that God is merciful and gracious. He forgives and continues to give us purpose.

I want to be clear that the fruit of the Spirit is one fruit that is displayed in several virtues. And this is what every believer is called to display—all of it. It is a part of our Christian discipleship. We can't major in one part and leave the others alone. I've heard people say, "I can be kind, but I can't forgive. I can love, but I can't be patient." The fruit of the Spirit is one fruit with differing aspects.

It's no surprise that what the Holy Spirit produces begins with love:

But the fruit of the Spirit is love, joy, peace, forbearance, kindness, goodness, faithfulness, gentleness and self-control. Against such things there is no law. Those who belong to Christ Jesus have crucified the flesh with its passions and desires. Since we live by the Spirit, let us keep in step with the Spirit. Let us not become conceited, provoking and envying each other. —Galatians 5:22–26

The fruit of the Spirit produces what is necessary for us to walk with God and to walk with one another. I get excited about this because it doesn't depend on me being perfect or never making a mistake. He is big enough to cover my mess-ups. I think about Peter. He was the disciple who made that bold statement recorded in Matthew 26:33: "Even if all fall away on account of you, I never will." He promised Jesus that no matter what anyone and everyone else did, he would never leave Him.

But just a few hours later, Peter denied three times that he even *knew* Jesus. I can only imagine his sorrow. I imagine that Peter must have felt deep in his heart, *I failed in the last minute, even though I was just with Him. I walked with Him. But I didn't love Him deeply enough.* But Jesus didn't leave Peter to wallow in his misery. After His resurrection, He met Peter at the Sea of Galilee and shared a meal with him. Three times He asked Peter if he loved Him. And finally He said to Peter, "Feed my sheep" (John 21:17). Even though Peter had denied Him, Jesus restored him and put him back on track to get to work for Him.

When I think about the war between the flesh and the spirit, it can seem overwhelming. As much as we want to do good, sometimes we fail. But I always remember that God is merciful and gracious. He forgives and continues to give us purpose. He continues to remind us that He has a plan for our lives. A plan for good and not for evil, to give us a hope and a future. I'm so glad about that.

## THE FRUIT OF THE SPIRIT IS LOVE

I want to spend the rest of this chapter talking about the fruit of the Spirit because that is what makes it possible for us to truly be friends with one another. I love it that the first idea presented is that of **love**. Love is affection, adoration, and compassion for others. It is not bound by lines of color, gender, or class. The love of Jesus is the motivating factor in the life of every believer. This is what the world needs so desperately, and it is what the Holy Spirit produces in our lives and hearts if we are friends of God.

I was walking through my office and the phone was ringing. I just happened to pick it up. A woman was on the line and she said, "I'm calling for my sister." I said, "I'm John Perkins here, who are you? Do you know that God loves you?" She immediately broke down on the phone. She wept. She didn't even know me. But she was having some problems, and just hearing that Jesus loved her was overwhelming. Thinking the connection was over, I was going to hang up, and she said, "No! Please don't hang up!" She didn't want me to stop telling her about Jesus. I said, "I don't care what you have done, Jesus Christ loves you!"

I so wanted her to know about the love of Jesus. That's the kind of love that will be with you through your life—no matter what. This is what hurting people need and He produces it in each of our hearts. He gives us the ability to love everybody no matter what they look like or where they come from. As much as lies within us, we must be intentional about reaching out and extending a hand to everyone. I'm praising Him for every opportunity to love like that! That's powerful. I didn't know that the phone was going to ring at that very moment. And I certainly didn't know that this lady was going to be calling. But He did. And when she spoke to me, it was a divine opportunity to make Jesus known.

## THE FRUIT OF THE SPIRIT IS JOY

The Holy Spirit also produces joy in our hearts. **Joy** is like a magnet that draws the eyes of the world. Pharrell Williams recorded a song a few years ago that took the music world by storm. It was called "Happy." It had a snappy beat to it and seemed to tap into what people needed. The world talks about being happy. The problem with happiness is that it depends on things happening the way you want them to. But the joy that the Holy Spirit produces doesn't depend on things happening a certain way. We can be full of joy in spite of very difficult circumstances. I'm always amazed when I think of Paul and Silas being in jail after being beaten for preaching the gospel. Scripture says that at midnight "Paul and Silas were praying and singing hymns to God, and the other prisoners were listening to them" (Acts 16:25). They were singing and praising God! Now, that's joy. They had been beaten and had no way of knowing what was going to happen to them the next day. Yet they were rejoicing.

> **What are the anchors of truth that you hold on to when life becomes hard?**

That must have seemed strange and unusual to the jailer. And when God shook the jail and set them free, Paul had the opportunity to share the gospel with the jailer and his family. They all became friends of God. I love that story because it says that if we can sing through a storm it may draw others to Jesus. They will want to know, *how is it that you can sing while you are going through something so terrible*? Those questions give us the opportunity to tell them about the wonderful love of Jesus that is available to them. Is your joy showing?

HE CALLS ME FRIEND

I think that Paul let us in on his secret of how to have joy in spite of everything that happens to us when he wrote Ephesians and said, "Therefore put on the full armor of God, so that when the day of evil comes, you may be able to stand your ground, and after you have done everything, to stand" (Eph. 6:13). We stand on the base of what we know and the convictions we have settled on. They are our reason for rejoicing.

Martin Luther, at the Diet of Worms, where the Roman Catholic Church challenged his convictions, is said to have declared, "Here I stand. I can do no other." I have a close friend who is on hospice care now. I call every day to see how he's doing. When I talked with him yesterday, he said, "I'm ready to meet my Maker." And he said it with joy. That joy came from a settled conviction that he will be with Jesus soon. That's joy! And it's always connected to a truth about Him. What are the anchors of truth that you hold on to when life becomes hard?

## THE FRUIT OF THE SPIRIT IS PEACE

Another important aspect of the fruit that the Holy Spirit produces in our hearts is peace. **Peace** is defined as: "Total well-being, prosperity, and security associated with God's presence among his people. . . . In the [New Testament], this longed-for peace is understood as having come in Christ and able to be experienced by faith."[5] Our peace rests in the character and person of Christ. People who are friends of God should be known as people of peace, not war. I've been so concerned as I look at what is happening in our country today. People have taken opposite sides in a political battle that has us at war with each other. This is the first time in my life we have made hate a virtue. I don't think we know the power of the words that have been unleashed in our culture today, and this even includes Christians warring against Christians! English Puritan William Gurnall said, "If the Gospel will not allow us to pay our enemies back in their own coin, returning anger for anger, then certainly it forbids a brother to spit fire into the face of another brother."[6]

The Holy Spirit helps us cross every man-made barrier to be at peace with one another. Even ethnic barriers? Yes, He helps us win the war of reconciliation. This battle has been my life blood, and I know that I cannot claim any credit for battles won. It has been His work through our hands that has accomplished whatever is good. He can cause us to remember that we have so much in common, in spite of our differences. Jesus taught His disciples, "Blessed are the peacemakers, for they will be called children of God" (Matt. 5:9). Peacemaking is a family trait in God's family. When God's children work for peace, we are demonstrating a family resemblance. We should all look like Jesus. We should all be peacemakers.

## THE FRUIT OF THE SPIRIT IS FORBEARANCE

The idea of **forbearance** is to withhold anger and to be patient with others. Jesus modeled this in His responses to His disciples again and again. He was patient with them when they could not stay awake and watch with Him in the garden of Gethsemane (see Matt. 26:36–46). He was patient with the Roman soldiers who gambled for His clothes and crucified Him, though He could have called a legion of angels to rescue Him. In the face of mistreatment, our fleshly response is to strike back quickly. That's kind of what people expect us to do. If somebody calls you an ethnic slur, you call them one back. If somebody curses at you, you curse back at them. If somebody hits you, you hit them back harder. But Jesus taught His followers that we are to live by a different standard. He said, "But I tell you, do not resist an evil person. If anyone slaps you on the right cheek, turn to them the other cheek also" (Matt. 5:39).

The Holy Spirit within us can give us the power to do that. This is what marked the civil rights movement and gave it uncommon power. It was the images of blacks and sympathetic whites who were willing to be beaten, spit on, and even killed without fighting back that drew the attention of the watching world. This kind of radical lifestyle is what the Holy Spirit empowers us to live. This example of patience in the face of evil gets the attention of the world and will provide opportunities for us to introduce others to Jesus.

## THE FRUIT OF THE SPIRIT IS KINDNESS AND GOODNESS

**Kindness** and **goodness** can be hard to put a finger on. They are best understood by what actions they produce. In the Old Testament when Boaz told his men to leave some sheaves of barley for Ruth to glean, Naomi said, "The LORD bless him! . . . He has not stopped showing his kindness to the living and the dead" (Ruth 2:20). Jesus showed great kindness as He dealt with children and those who lived on the margins of society. The opposite of kindness is abusive, harsh, rude.

In Luke 6:34–35, Jesus tells His disciples to do good to everyone, even their enemies. By doing this we look like God our Father who is "kind to the ungrateful and wicked." Can you imagine what our world would be like if all of us who are followers and friends of Jesus would put this into practice? It would be a huge contrast with the mean-spiritedness and harsh words that are common today. I believe that we could turn the world upside down with deeds of kindness and goodness that would point people to Jesus.

## THE FRUIT OF THE SPIRIT IS FAITHFULNESS

**Faithfulness** is "the character of one who can be relied on; . . . of one who keeps his promises."[7] Jesus modeled faithfulness throughout His earthly life. The writer of Hebrews said that "Jesus Christ is the same yesterday and today and forever" (13:8). He did not change His character depending on which group He was with. He didn't change His purpose because the political winds shifted. He was faithful.

I can't think of many things that are more needed today than for our words to mean what we say and for people to be able to depend on us to not be phony or shifty. For a promise made to be a promise kept. This is crucial to healthy friendships, and it is really important in the forming of new friendships and relationships. Broken promises can easily derail friendships. But we can be grateful for the work of the Holy Spirit in our lives. He helps us honor our words and be faithful stewards of what we have spoken.

## THE FRUIT OF THE SPIRIT IS GENTLENESS

**Gentleness** is mildness, meekness, humility. It's pretty hard to find this quality on display today. Our culture applauds people who are brash and arrogant. The self-promoter gets the most attention and the most encouragement. But God intends for His friends to be marked by gentleness. Oswald Sanders shared this quote from Robert Morrison in *Spiritual Leadership*: "The great fault, I think, in our mission is that no one likes to be second," and Sanders went on to add: "The world has yet to see what could happen if everyone lost the desire to get the glory. Wouldn't it be a marvelous place if nobody cared who got the credit?"[8]

The opposite of gentleness, meekness, and humility is

pride. Pride pushes people away and makes it hard for us to cross the barrier to friendship. I'm constantly aware of this inner struggle. I don't want to get in the way of what the Holy Spirit is trying to do in my heart.

## THE FRUIT OF THE SPIRIT IS SELF-CONTROL

**Self-control** is self-restraint proceeding out from *within* oneself, but *not by oneself*. For the believer, "self-control, Spirit-control" can only be accomplished *by the power of the Lord*.[9] To be under the Spirit's control is to be filled by Him. I think a lot of misdirected people have the idea that this is just an emotional deal. But being filled with the Holy Spirit is to be controlled by Him.

A story was told about a time when D. L. Moody was speaking to a large audience. Holding up a glass, he asked, "How can I get the air out of this glass?" One man shouted, "Suck it out with a pump!" Moody replied, "That would create a vacuum and shatter the glass." After numerous other suggestions, Moody smiled, picked up a pitcher of water, and filled the glass. "There," he said, "all the air is now removed." He then went on to explain that victory in the Christian life is not accomplished by "sucking out a sin here and there" but by being filled with the Holy Spirit.[10] When we are filled with the Holy Spirit, He controls all of us. It's all of Him and none of me.

Bill Bright, founder of Campus Crusade for Christ, shares three steps to being filled with the Holy Spirit.[11]

1. We must desire to live a life that pleases Him. He promises that if we hunger and thirst for Him, He will fill us with His righteousness.

2. We must be willing to surrender totally to Him. In Romans 12, Paul encourages us to offer our bodies as a living sacrifice to

Him. That means we are dead to our selfish ways.

3. We must ask the Holy Spirit to bring to our remembrance any unconfessed sin. "If we confess our sins, he is faithful and just and will forgive us our sins and purify us from all unrighteousness" (1 John 1:9).

## THE HOLY SPIRIT IS RELIABLE

I often find myself rolling out of bed in the middle of the night and feeling like I've got to come before Him in prayer. I think a lot of people believe that prayer is just talking to God; but it's more than that. I listen for His voice, and He reminds me of what He has said in His Word. I'm seeking Him for the strength that I don't have because I have come to the end of myself, and He always provides exactly what I need.

We can all be encouraged because the fruit of the Spirit—love, joy, peace, forbearance, kindness, goodness, gentleness, self-control—are all His work. We don't have to grit our teeth and use self-effort to develop the fruit. But we do need to cooperate with Him as He prompts us and speaks to us through the Word and through circumstances. And He is ever speaking.

> I think a lot of people believe that prayer is just talking to God; but it's more than that. I listen for His voice, and He reminds me of what He has said in His Word.

A former park ranger at Yellowstone National Park tells the story of a ranger leading a group of hikers to a fire lookout. The ranger was so intent on telling the hikers about the flowers and animals that he considered the messages on his two-way radio distracting, so he switched it off. Nearing the tower, the ranger was met by a nearly breathless lookout, who asked why he hadn't responded to the messages on his radio. A grizzly bear had been seen stalking the group, and the authorities were trying to warn them of the danger. Any time we tune out the messages God has sent us, we put at peril not only ourselves, but also those around us.[12]

The Holy Spirit is speaking. And what He is doing in the hearts of everyone who belongs to God is an inside job. He gives us spiritual gifts to develop in service to others. Romans 12 and 1 Corinthians 12 provide a list of the spiritual gifts. Every believer has as least one gift and no one has all of the gifts. He intends for us to know that we need one another in this Christian walk.

The Holy Spirit is equipping us to know God and to make Him known. He is reproducing the character of Christ in each of us. He is giving us the ability to love the tax collector, the prostitute, and the leper, just as Jesus did. He is prodding us to cross every barrier known to mankind to make friends and help others come to know our God. We'll talk about making friends with others in the next chapter, but I'm overjoyed to have you hear from a special friend who has been like the Holy Spirit in my life for more than thirty years. He has been with me through good times and bad times. Through the sun and the rain. I hope you'll be encouraged by Wayne Gordon's story.

Let's Hear It from Wayne Gordon:

# *Friendship*
# MEANS GOING DEEP

I remember hearing John Perkins speak in chapel at Wheaton College my senior year. When he was done speaking, my heart was filled with a sense of, *Yes, he's talking about what You, God, have called me to do.* From that very moment, John Perkins became a hero to me. The next year he wrote the book *Let Justice Roll Down.* I read it immediately and began my lifelong privilege of learning from John Perkins.

Now that would be enough in itself. But I'm thankful to God that my wife, Anne, and I were able to go to Jubilee '82 in Jackson, Mississippi. John Perkins and others from Voice of Calvary ministry sponsored it. This was where we met John personally. I first remember a brief conversation with him and telling him a little bit of what we were doing in Lawndale. That began the process of him moving from hero to a major influencer in my life: from teacher, then becoming my mentor, coworker, colleague, friend—and now best friend. Now we are soul mates for life. We have the privilege of talking on the phone almost every day. In fact, today I've talked to him twice.

John agreed to be on the advisory board for Lawndale Community Church and advise us as we were striving to have a ministry here in Chicago. One day I got a call from John and he said he was coming to preach at Moody Bible Institute. He asked if I could pick him up at the airport. He had a couple extra hours and would come by and see what we were doing here in Lawndale. I remember that day so vividly. It was before the days of heavy security at airports, and I was able to go to the gate. Looking around I kept thinking, *Surely somebody else is going to be here to pick him up. There's no way I get to pick up John Perkins at the airport!* Yet when he got off the plane, I recognized him immediately and went up to him. No one else was there to pick him up! It was me.

I drove him back to our community of North Lawn-dale on Chicago's West Side and showed him around, sharing some of our dreams. John likes to reflect that there was nothing there but a lot of talk. Anne had prepared lunch for us, so we went over to our apartment for lunch. We talked together and John began the process of mentoring Anne and me in our work here in Chicago.

For the next four to five years, I heard John speak or met with him two to three times a year. It was the beginning of us having our hearts knit together because of our common purpose of making a difference in urban America. We began to hold urban ministry training seminars during our board meetings in the fall of each year. John was always one of the keynote speakers who not only helped me learn from him but others from our church and also others in Chicago.

It was in the late '80s that we began to talk about expanding these urban ministry conferences to becoming a national association. This was the start of the Christian Community Development Association (CCDA) for people like us who were doing ministry around the nation in urban areas. John became the chairman of the board and I the first president of CCDA. We continued to lead together for the next twenty-five years.

During this time John and I had the privilege of traveling together beginning in 1995. We have gone to over a hundred cities to do weekend seminars. Our habit was to stay together in the same hotel room, which allowed us to talk throughout our time together. This is when our relationship moved from being a mentor, to coworkers and colleagues.

For the last thirty-five years, almost always when John is in Chicago, he stays in our home. This has allowed him to become very close to my whole family. My children call him Grandpa Perkins. He and Anne have an extremely special relationship that's deep and unique in itself. JP gets up early and always has a fresh new thought on his mind. He is always seeking the truth, and it's fun to be with him with his first thoughts in the morning. Anne has always competed with me to be the first one to see John in the morning so she could get his new fresh thought.

One of the things that I've appreciated so much about JP is that he is very concerned about me personally. We ask each other the hard questions and are able to look each other deep in our soul. We often find ourselves completing one another's sentences. It's in JP seeking the truth that our relationship has been built.

It is through common ministry and common purpose that John and I have grown deeper and deeper in our love for each other. I am so thankful for the tremendous blessing having this deep friendship with JP is. I love the way we love each other and encourage each other daily. I hold this so tenderly with great privilege and deep value. I know he calls many people his best friend. I have heard him refer to other people in that way countless times. That's the nature of who he is. Whoever he is with at that moment is his best friend. I'm thankful to at least be one of those "best friends."

Wayne "Coach" Gordon

*Wayne Gordon is pastor of Lawndale Community Church and chairman/president of Christian Community Development Association. He makes his home in Chicago, IL.*

# Part Four

# FRIENDSHIP WITH OTHERS

"*Friendship is born at that moment when one person says to another, 'What! You too? I thought I was the only one.'*"

C. S. Lewis

# CHAPTER 8

# Crossing Hard Lines

*For the past few years, nine-year-old Chase Hansen has sat down with homeless people to find out how to help them. As a young child, Chase first saw homeless people. He and his father, John, started Project Empathy—a one-on-one meal between a homeless person and a non-homeless person. They listen to the person's story and find out how they can help. In Chase's words: "Project Empathy is supposed to help them get a friend and help them move forward, to get a job and learn life principles and what they can do better." One man they were able to help is their friend Justin, who said, "They've helped me a lot first, in seeing that I have self-worth."[1]*

Chase, who has been given a service award by the governor of Utah, has a multitude of new friends because he saw their need and cared enough to respond. I love this story. It gives me hope. And it reminds me that sometimes we need to see the world through the eyes of a child. A child who hasn't been scarred and tainted by all of the barriers and boundary lines we put up to say, *don't go there; don't talk to them.* Sometimes we need a child to lead us across those hard lines.

## FRIENDSHIP BEGINS WITH THE OTHER

People always ask me, "John, how do you become friends?" The first thing is to know and understand the other. The first thing people want to talk about is a program. You don't start with a program; you start with the people and what they bring. Then that bond ties them together. The program comes out of what it is they want to do. What I want to do may be entirely different from what is really needed.

We have a felt-need concept with the Christian Community Development Association (CCDA). This is the way to find that mutual need that binds us together without dehumanizing us but by affirming each other's dignity. You have to find a person's deepest longing and need. We used the words of this poem to guide our efforts:

> Go to the people, live among them, learn from them, love them. Start with what they know, build on what they have: But of the best leaders, when their task is done, the people will remark, "We have done it ourselves."[2]

Friendship with others is commanded in Scripture. Jesus taught that we were to love our neighbors as ourselves. When a young man questioned who his neighbor was, Jesus responded by telling him the story of the Good Samaritan. We can learn a lot from this story in Luke 10:30–37 about how to become a friend with a stranger:

> Jesus said: "A man was going down from Jerusalem to Jericho, when he was attacked by robbers. They stripped him of his clothes, beat him and went away, leaving him half dead. A priest happened to be going down the same

road, and when he saw the man, he passed by on the other side. So too, a Levite, when he came to the place and saw him, passed by on the other side. But a Samaritan, as he traveled, came where the man was; and when he saw him, he took pity on him. He went to him and bandaged his wounds, pouring on oil and wine. Then he put the man on his own donkey, brought him to an inn and took care of him. The next day he took out two denarii [two days' wages] and gave them to the innkeeper. 'Look after him,' he said, 'and when I return, I will reimburse you for any extra expense you may have.'

"Which of these three do you think was a neighbor to the man who fell into the hands of robbers?"

The expert in the law replied, "The one who had mercy on him."

Jesus told him, "Go and do likewise."

The Samaritan became a friend of the man who had been beaten because he saw his need. He had compassion on him and he met his need—just as Jesus would have done. His response was totally different from the priest's and the Levite's responses. They both were religious men. There's been a lot of discussion about why they would have passed by instead of stopping to help. What it boils down to, it seems, is that their religious rules kept them from caring enough to help.

If our religion keeps us from helping people in need, it's probably the wrong kind of religion. If our religion allows us to look at people who are hurting and in desperate need and then walk around them without helping, something is wrong. Not caring is not an option if we are friends of God and if the Holy Spirit is reproducing the character of Christ in our hearts and lives. Not caring, for someone who is a friend of God, is like not breathing. We have to breathe to survive. And we have to care to survive—because caring is what makes us alive spiritually. It stokes the fires of passion in our hearts and it becomes a magnet that beckons others.

I can't see other people hurting and look the other way. I'm not made up like that. My heart breaks when I see their pain. Passion means entering into the pain and hurt of other people. And I think that's what Jesus is looking for us to do. When we walked the streets of Mendenhall, Mississippi, many years ago helping people get registered to vote, we drove through the countryside and sat with people in their cramped shanties. Our hearts ached for their need for decent housing. That stirring in our hearts led to the first black housing development in that area. At every turn, whenever we saw a need, we were compelled to do whatever we could to minister to that need.

We wanted to be like the Good Samaritan whenever we saw a need. We wanted to be the hands and feet of Jesus for people who were hurting. I remember a woman whose son was living in Chicago. He had become so sick that doctors didn't expect him to live much longer. But for his mother, she wanted nothing more than to see her son one more time and bring him back to Mississippi before he died. Getting on a train or any kind of public transportation at that time was out of the question, because of the cost and the concern for a woman traveling alone through the South. So we drove her to Chicago to get her son and brought him back to Mississippi. I can't put into words the joy on that mother's face to see her son one more time, to hold him one more time. I learned a lot about what it means to enter into the pain of someone else. Their pain becomes our pain. Their joy becomes our joy.

Our world today is full of hurting people. You almost have to have a blindfold on to avoid seeing them when you walk the streets. They are the homeless. They are the ladies of the night. They are the young people without purpose who stalk our streets. They are the drug dealers and the addicted. They are the outcasts of our day . . . the very people Jesus would be sharing a meal with and spending His time with. They are people who are on the other side of hard lines that we have drawn. Sometimes those hard lines have to do with class or religion. Other times those lines are all about color of skin.

## FRIENDSHIP CROSSES COLOR LINES

I have learned that friendship can take us across ethnic barriers even into Ku Klux Klan territory. My friend Tommy Tarrants was a former Klan member. He opposed desegregation in the South, and this man known as "the most dangerous man in Mississippi" was blamed for many of the bombings there, which targeted churches and synagogues. He was arrested and sent to prison. While in prison he read the Gospels and had a life-changing conversion. What he read convinced him that racism was wrong: "There is neither Jew nor Gentile, neither slave nor free, nor is there male and female, for you are all one in

> We've drawn some hard lines in our country today. They are racial, they are political. They are ugly. They are wrong. If we are friends of God and if the Spirit of God lives in our hearts, we must renounce bigotry and political prejudice.

Christ Jesus" (Gal. 3:28). He renounced the Klan and devoted his life to serving Christ and promoting the peace that only Christ can give.

Tommy and I met for the first time when we were both invited to speak at Geneva College in the fall of 1990. I wasn't sure whether to believe that he had really changed. So I brought him into a room filled with black college students where I was to speak. But instead I invited Tommy to speak. I wanted to see if the students would believe that he had changed.

Tommy said, "I was raised in Mobile, Alabama, in the 1960s. I was a churchgoing kid. I was baptized. I thought I was a Christian. I believed that blacks were inferior to whites and that Jews, who were promoting integration, were the source of all evil. Eventually that began to spill over into violence. . . . But God changed my heart and gave me an attitude of love toward people."[3] He encouraged the students to "have a friend of a different race and get to know that person as a friend and understand what life is like for them."[4] *The Preacher and the Klansman* tells our story of friendship; and we later wrote *He's My Brother: Former Racial Foes Offer Strategy for Reconciliation.*[5] Tommy is now the president of the C. S. Lewis Institute in Washington, D.C. I share this story because if extreme cases of bigotry can be destroyed through friendship, then there is no excuse for blacks, whites, Hispanics, Asians, native Americans, and everyone else not to be able to make the journey to friendship.

We've drawn some hard lines in our country today. They are racial, they are political. They are ugly. They are wrong. If we are friends of God and if the Spirit of God lives in our hearts, we must renounce bigotry and political prejudice. We should have friends who are Republican, who are Democrats, who are Independents. We should have friends who look like every ethnicity under heaven. Why would we want to go to heaven where every tribe and every tongue will be worshiping together at the feet of our God if we don't want to be friends with everyone now?

## FRIENDSHIP CAN BE MENTORING

Friendship can be based on need as it was for Chase's friends. It can cause us to cross ethnic lines and class lines, as it did for me and Tommy. But it can also be seen as mentoring. When I think about mentoring, I reflect on how the apostle Paul wrote to his sons in the ministry, Timothy and Titus. He gave them guidelines for what it means to be a leader. He told them to not be afraid to be bold for the Lord and to not be discouraged because they were young. There was a lot that they needed to know, and he was equipped to teach them.

Mordecai was an Old Testament figure who mentored his young cousin Esther as if she were his own daughter. His counsel positioned her to become queen of Persia. And when their people, the Jews, were threatened with being wiped out, he reminded her that God had placed her in the palace so she could help her people. When it seemed like she wasn't hearing him, he gave her some hard words that basically said, "If you don't come through for your people, God will provide salvation through someone else." His words of wisdom helped her see the situation differently and she determined to appeal to the king for her people, even in light of personal risk. She said, "If I perish, I perish." (Est. 4:16). But those words were spoken because of the counsel of a strong mentor and friend. Friendship can be like that. It can be mentoring.

I have been blessed to have had some wonderful mentors who spoke into my life early on and kept me moving in the right direction. One of those special friends and mentors was Mr. R. A. Buckley. He was the smartest human being I ever met. He had a modest background, but he was brilliant. He joined the church in Mendenhall when I came back, and he became the father I never had. He would tell me, "Be a good father." But I didn't know what that meant. He said, "You *got* to be a *better* father."

I went to pick him up one day and give him a ride into town. I had a young woman in my car I needed to talk with about the civil rights movement. I had this young woman in the car with me for the ten minutes it took to drive out to the country to pick up Mr. Buckley. He said I should not have been alone in a car with a woman. He insisted, "Never do that again. Never do that again!" I didn't ever do that again.

Momma Wilson in California became the mother I never had. This was right after I was converted. She had one son and she was discipling me. In fact, she told me that I was discipling her. She said I taught the Bible like she had never heard it taught before. I tried not to let that go to my head, because you don't ever get smarter than your momma. She will slap you down—in love. She taught me how to live. I had left California for a time, and while I was away her only son was killed in a car accident. When I came back to California, she took all the love she had for her one son and poured that love out on me. Her love was healing for me. Her mentoring kind of friendship helped me in my preaching and in my living.

And I remember Mrs. James. She became a great friend of Vera Mae. She used to be my secretary and was a retired school-teacher. She was in her seventies then, and she also became like a momma to me. We had a Bible class early in the morning. It started off as my staff Bible class, and then I began to invite others to come. All of a sudden a lot of women started coming to the class. Mrs. James was a wise woman and nothing got by me without her seeing it. When the class was over, I was so pleased. I was so happy that all these women were coming. I said, "Oh! The Bible class was really good today!" Mrs. James said, "They ain't coming for Bible class!" I said, "What are they coming for?" She said, "They're coming up in here with their dresses all short and tight. They're coming to get you!" We had just come to town and were still learning our way. Everywhere we went we tried to start a Bible class. Mrs. James was a true mentor. She helped me set my values. I learned a lot

> **Real joy is passing on what you know and making friends with young folks.**

about where to draw lines. I learned the wisdom of keeping doors open and having glass doors that people can see through. Today, too many people don't have those kinds of mentors in their lives. We've got to nurture people. We've got to go deeper in friendship. We've got to be willing to risk speaking up when we see folks moving in the wrong direction.

When I think of mentoring as a kind of friendship, I think of all of the teachers across the country who interact with children every day. What an opportunity to speak words of encouragement, love, and friendship into the lives and hearts of these young people!

In the 1920s, a sociology class at Johns Hopkins University made a study of children in deprived neighborhoods in Baltimore. They identified two hundred children who appeared doomed to spend years in prison. After twenty-five years, another study was made to discover what had happened to those particular children. Surprisingly, only two were incarcerated. As these men and women were interviewed over and over again came the name of their teacher, "Aunt Hannah." The sociologists were correct in their predictions. By all indications the children would be dregs of society; but there was an intervention, Aunt Hannah, an elementary schoolteacher who loved them.[6]

Every single teacher in America has the opportunity and privilege to be the "Aunt Hannah" in the lives of the children they teach. Just a smile, just a word of encouragement, just an offer of friendship and love can change the direction of a life. My heart breaks for the scores of young people today who think that nobody cares about them. We can change that through friendship.

I think of parents who have raised their children and now can help mentor young couples, and of young adults who can be big brothers and big sisters to children who need guidance. These are examples of friendships waiting to happen. There is no end to the opportunities we have to mentor others and become friends. Mr. Buckley had learned how to be a good husband and he had raised twelve children, so he could pass that knowledge on to me. I hope that those of us who are senior citizens can see that we have so much to pass on to the next generation. We could spend a lot of time doing things to just enjoy life, like traveling to casinos or hanging out in the barber shop. But real joy is passing on what you know and making friends with young folks. What have you learned that you can pass on to someone else who needs to be mentored and who needs a friend?

The idea of making friends can be scary. It seems hard. In the next chapter we'll talk about some simple steps to take in being friends, making friends, going deep into friendship. But before we do that, let's remind ourselves that we all have the best friend in the world in Jesus. We are not friendless. We have a friend in Jesus, and He gives us everything we need to reach across every barrier—even the barrier of our own fear—and reproduce friendships everywhere we go. I know this is true, because He has been gracious in doing this in and through my own life.

"Walking with a friend in the dark is better than walking alone in the light."

———

Helen Keller

# CHAPTER 9

# The Friendship Challenge

*Two are better than one, because they have a good return for their labor: If either of them falls down, one can help the other up. But pity anyone who falls and has no one to help them up. Also, if two lie down together, they will keep warm. But how can one keep warm alone? Though one may be overpowered, two can defend themselves. A cord of three strands is not quickly broken. (Eccl. 4:9–12)*

Those words were written by Solomon, who was known as the wisest man who ever lived. He seems to say that friendship is a crucial need for every human being. And the Lord agreed. From the very beginning He said, "It is not good for man to be alone." The craving for friendship and for connection was meant to draw us to one another. I think God gave us a deep longing to be loved; it's sort of a pain in your heart. I don't know . . . maybe we hurt and hate others out of that pain if it isn't tended to. It's a deep need.

That's really the essence of life. Life that matters. The good life. It's not about money, fame, or possessions. It's a life filled with friendships. Friendship with God and friendships with others. Friendships that cross ethnic, gender, and class lines.

What would the world look like if we traded in our pursuit of the American dream for friendship with God and friendship with others? What if the aching in our souls could finally be filled through friendships?

We desperately need one another in order to be fully human and to fully reflect the character of God. But we can't reflect the character of God if we don't know Him. He invites us to friendship with Himself first. He is the most important friend you will ever have. If you have never accepted Him as Savior and friend, I invite you to pray this prayer right now:

> Lord, thank You for pursuing me and revealing Yourself to me as Savior and Friend. Thank You for dying on the cross to save me from my sins. I open the door of my heart and receive You as Savior and Lord. Please take control of my life and show me how to live as Your friend in this world. Thank You that I will never be alone.

If you just prayed that prayer, you can be confident that He now lives within your heart and He will direct your life. When I came to know this God as Savior and Friend, it was the answer to the deep longing in my heart. I pray that it will be like that for you too, and that you will share what has happened with someone else. Then pray and ask God to lead you to a small group or a church where you can grow in your relationship with Him.

For every one of us who is a friend of God, we have the privilege and responsibility to make Him known and to become friends with others. God the Father, God the Son, and God the Holy Spirit have modeled the key aspects of friendship for us: pursue, go deep, forgive, cross lines, be with, bear fruit. Let's talk about how we can put each of these into practice.

## FRIENDSHIP PURSUES

God set His gaze on every one of us and pursued us until we were captured by His love. There's something about that that goes deep. He fixed His eyes on us. It was not a fleeting glance. People need to see their worth and dignity reflected in our eyes. We miss countless opportunities when we look past people and refuse to see their eyes. This is the first step. We must do for others what He did for us, and we must be intentional about it. When we realize deep down what God did to pursue us when we were far from Him, we'll be motivated to tell others about Him. Our world is full of lonely people . . . and they come in many colors. Loneliness is no respecter of persons.

Every day offers an opportunity to engage with others in loving ways that draw them into friendship. It takes purpose and effort. And it takes prayer. We need the Lord to open our eyes to see the loneliness that shrouds the faces of people we meet. And we need Him to give us a heart to care and to reach out with the offer of friendship. For those of us who find it difficult to make the first move, we need Him to give us courage and determination. We can pray for this courage and watch Him work in our lives to make us more and more open to initiating friendships.

And then we need to act. Watch for a new person who comes to your church. Be sure to greet them and that they know where to go; point them to the coffee table, if your church has one. If they have children, direct them to the children's department. Find out if they'd like an invitation to lunch. Let them know of ministries your church offers such as small groups or Bible studies. These are great places to form relationships and to break down the barriers that often divide us even in church.

Arrive early at meetings or worship services and use the

time to talk to people you wouldn't normally talk to. Plan to stay after the meeting ends to interact with people. Sit with a senior citizen and see how you can help them. Make yourself available as a helper to a young mother who has children she's trying to keep up with. Encourage a young boy who's growing up without a father. Take a walk through your neighborhood and talk to the young people. Encourage them to stay in school and to do well. Ask for their names and remember them.

At the end of the day, assess how you interacted with the people God brought to you. Are there potential friends who you can begin praying for?

## FRIENDSHIP GOES DEEP

God had face-to-face friendship with Moses. He had intimate friendship with Abraham. They came to know Him because He revealed Himself and His heart to them. Everybody says this is really hard for men to do, harder for men than for women; but we've got to change this thing. We've got to risk going deeper than just hello and goodbye. We must be willing to become a learner about the other and to share our own hearts.

A new study done by Harvard University researchers discovered that people really like talking about themselves. Talking about yourself stimulates the same areas of the brain that light up when enjoying good food or experiencing other pleasant triggers. People get a "neurological buzz" when they talk about themselves.[1] One study says, "That's why we spend almost 40 percent of conversation talking about ourselves— our brain chemistry drives us to do it."[2] If the research is accurate, then it should not be difficult to begin new friendships . . . just get people talking about themselves. And listen carefully to what they say. Make a note of what they say and pray over it. The next time you see them, refer to something that they shared with you and let them know you have been praying for them. Begin to share your life in increasing measure with each interaction.

A lot of us may feel like Shauna Niequist: "I've spent most of my life and most of my friendships holding my breath and hoping that when people get close enough they won't leave, and fearing that it's a matter of time before they figure me out and go."[3] This fear is real and it can keep many of us from going deep in friendship. I encourage you to risk sharing your heart. Focus on being a friend more than finding a friend. Be a good listener and share honestly.

## FRIENDSHIP FORGIVES

Friendship can be messy business because people can hurt us. The Lord's Prayer reminds us that we should forgive others in the same way we expect God to forgive us. People make mistakes, so if you choose not to forgive every time someone offends you, then your life will be pretty lonely. You can't be in relationship with people and avoid being hurt. But God gives us the heart to forgive no matter what the hurt is. The Holy Spirit, who lives within, shows us how to see our offender through the eyes of Christ and to show mercy toward them—just as He shows mercy to us every time we offend Him by our sin.

Scripture tells us not to let the sun go down on our wrath. But in our own self-righteousness we sit back and wait for the other person to beg us for forgiveness. If I say anything that brings up my brokenness in the wrong way, some of my friends say, "Oh! Don't say that! You've grown past that!" I may be actually in need of help, but they have exalted me so that I can't ask for help. I remind them that none of us is righteous. We stand in His righteousness alone. And we all need His help to forgive ourselves and to forgive others.

We don't see our own brokenness nearly as quickly as we see that of others. We don't see what we've done wrong when our friendships fall apart. We walk away from friendships that can become meaningful and rich because we refuse to forgive hurts. My heart aches when I remember my father walking away from me when I was a small child. I think that's why I don't easily break off relationships now, even when people try to poison my mind against someone because they don't like them. Early in my life, if I felt like someone was just too bad, I would make them a nonperson, an "empty suit," and they would cease to exist for me. There are some graves that I wish I could go back and dig up. I've learned the hard way that every potential friend can become a better friend if I don't give up.

Are there people who you need to go back and get? Maybe a friend who hurt you in the past can become a better friend if you forgive and give them another chance. Ask the Lord for direction on what you should do . . . and then obey.

## FRIENDSHIP CROSSES LINES

Jesus showed us how to cross lines. He made Himself vulnerable. He did not condemn. And He always affirmed the dignity of the other. We must be honest about the lines we have drawn. Who are the ones that you don't associate with? Are they poor people . . . rich people? Are they black people . . . white people? Are they educated people . . . uneducated people? Are they Democrats . . . Republicans? Are they Christians . . . atheists? If you are a friend of God and the character of Christ is being developed in your heart, the lines represent sin. We must cross every line, just as Jesus did. We must offer friendship and love. We must make Him known by our actions.

God always keeps the relationship bigger than the problem. That's what friendship does. We may have friends who are on the other side of the fence politically, but we're able to keep that friendship

> **God always keeps the relationship bigger than the problem. That's what friendship does.**

because we're going to keep the relationship bigger than politics. Most of my friends became friends around some type of disagreement between us. There were lines drawn that had to be crossed. There's probably no topic that is more open to disagreement than that of reconciliation. It's been my life's work, and for me this issue has provided opportunities for discussion and negotiation. It's in that negotiation that we become friends. I say, "We may see things differently, but basically we believe the same thing." And another friendship is born.

A KKK member and a black man can become friends when they realize that they both want the same things. They both want the world to be a safe place for their families; and they want life to be better for their children. Since we all want the same things, these common goals can serve as a basis for friendship.

We can pray for God's blessings on those we have felt separated from and for their hearts to be softened even as ours are. We can pray for opportunities to engage with them in new ways and for a new spirit of friendship and brotherhood to develop. We can pray that we will not become discouraged if our first try at reaching out does not work. We will all need the Lord to keep us moving forward and to not give up when we are rejected and things don't go the way we want them to.

HE CALLS ME FRIEND

## FRIENDSHIP IS "BEING WITH"

Jesus was with His disciples for more than three years before He died on the cross. He ate, slept, and did the work He came to do *with* them. After He went back to heaven, He left the Holy Spirit to be with us forever. He is our forever Friend. You can't get around the concept of togetherness when you talk about how to be friends. Friendship is time spent together. It's meeting at a coffee shop once a week and then taking the friendship to a deeper level by sharing a meal in one another's home. It's going to sporting events together and finding common ground to build a friendship on.

When I meet with and teach young people, I often ask them, *What do you like about yourself?* At first they don't want to answer because it seems like they'd be bragging. When they start answering, do you know what they usually say? It's *helping somebody*. That's how they respond 99 percent of the time. They like knowing that they can help somebody else. That they can make somebody else happy. Most of them just need somebody to spend time with them and help channel that passion and energy. We need to spend time with them. They can change the world. They can make a difference.

With the Christian Community Development Association (CCDA) we took this idea of being "with" very seriously. We believe in relocation. We went where the brokenness was. We lived among the people in some of America's neediest neighborhoods. A goal is to "become one with our neighbors until there is no longer an 'us' and 'them,' but only a 'we.'"[4] Being with is an investment of time and heart.

## FRIENDSHIP BEARS FRUIT

The Holy Spirit comes into our empty hearts and begins developing the character of Christ within. Where there was hatred and bigotry, He sows love. Where there was anger and resentment, He sows forgiveness and kindness. He makes us better. He makes us fruitful. And this is our challenge as we meet lonely people every day—people who are wallowing in hatred, anger, bitterness. Our offer of friendship, our offer of Christ to them can change their lives forever. Paul reminded the Corinthian believers that God had reconciled them to Himself, and then gave them the task of making peace with others. (See 2 Cor. 5:18.)

> This has been my greatest privilege—to make more friends everywhere I go, and to be enriched by friends who have stayed with me through the ups and downs of my journey.

All people need the same thing we needed before we knew the Lord: to know Jesus as Savior and Friend. He is the answer to the longing in their hearts. He fixes our sin problem and He transforms our lives with His love and purpose. It is our joy and privilege to introduce Him to our friends. We can pray and ask the Lord to provide the right opportunity for this. Sometimes the door is opened after a person has a difficult life experience. Other times how we handle our own troubles causes our friends to ask how we're able to stand strong and keep from giving up.

These are opportunities to tell them that Jesus makes the difference in our lives. The apostle Peter encourages us: "Always be prepared to give an answer to everyone who asks you to give the reason for the hope that you have" (1 Peter 3:15b).

As we pass people in our daily lives, we can pray and ask the Lord to show us how to reach them for Him. He can show us a need we can fill, a question we can ask, help we can offer. These can be the first steps toward friendship.

Deep in my heart I really believe that this is what the Lord desires of us: that we would stop running after more stuff, more money, more of the things that never satisfy and apply ourselves to the Friendship Challenge. Pursue . . . Go Deep . . . Forgive . . . Cross Lines . . . Be With . . . Bear Fruit. This has been my greatest privilege—to make more friends everywhere I go, and to be enriched by friends who have stayed with me through the ups and downs of my journey. I can truly agree with these words by Hubert H. Humphrey: "The greatest gift of life is friendship, and I have received it."[5]

In this section we've talked about friendship as mentorship. I count it an undeserved privilege to be a father and to be able to walk before my children as best I can. To be a father is enough. But to be able to cross over from father to friend with your children is the greatest gift of all. My son, Phillip, will share this last friendship letter.

Let's Hear It from Phillip Perkins:

# My Daddy, MY FRIEND

My dad and I have had a special bond ever since I was a little boy. When I was as young as three years old, if I heard his car cranking up I would run downstairs as fast as I could, shouting, "Daddy! Daddy! Can I go?"

He would always say yes. He never said no. He would take me with him, and it was always the two of us—even though I had two older brothers and other siblings. When my parents had discussions and would disagree, I always took Daddy's side. If he wanted it, I wanted it. Our relationship helped shape the kind of father I am with my two sons.

I was aware as I grew up that he wasn't just working for his own children, he was working for the whole community. So a lot of times he didn't get to be with us because he made a sacrifice for the community and for blacks in Mississippi. He believed in the inherent dignity of every person, so we went to white schools before

155

integration became mandatory. He stood for something.

He doesn't like to talk about what happened when he was brutally beaten in the Brandon jail after being arrested for standing up for the rights of our people. But I was forever marked by what I saw and what I heard. There were two vans of students from Tougaloo College and Jackson State University who were coming to join the march for justice. The vans were stopped and everybody was arrested, except one white female student from Philadelphia. I remember sitting on the staircase listening to the conversation in our living room when the telephone rang. The student was calling for my dad. She was hysterical as she begged him to get to the jail right away.

A few of the men at the house went with him. He couldn't have known that what he was walking into was going to be as torturous as it was—but I believe he would have gone anyway. I didn't see him until a week later . . . after he got out of jail. When I saw him for the first time after the beating he was coming across the lawn and I was throwing a football. He looked at me and I looked at him. He was so messed up. He had knots on his head that were two to three inches tall and as round as a tennis ball. His whole face was bruised, and you could not see any whites in his eyes. They were all red. They were bloodshot. He looked at me, and he had an embarrassed look on his face. He never stopped walking. He had the eye of the tiger.

In spite of how weak he was, he was determined to lead another march, standing up for our rights. As we took off on the march, I was on the second row. We could hear the ladies who came out of their houses screaming, "Ya'll gonna get killed!" I was so afraid. When we turned

156

the corner, I thought that I saw a gun. I wanted to run, but the closer I got, I saw that it was a news camera. They brought a pickup truck. Daddy got up on the pickup truck and made a powerful speech. The police were standing in riot gear with guns across their chests. He pointed at them and said, "They tried to kill me, but the Lord wasn't ready for me yet! All we want is the same thing they want. We want good schools for our children. We want good jobs so we can take care of our families." Cold chills went through my body as I stood close by.

As I watched my dad, the question that went through my mind was, *What would drive a man to do this?* Then I asked myself, *Could I do this?* I don't really know. You never know until you're faced with a situation how you'll respond. I could never be upset with my dad more than just a little bit, because of what he sacrificed for us.

He has marked my life in so many ways. I wanted to be a minister or a politician to help straighten out the stuff that's going on in our country. I became the minister but not the politician. I've learned so many life lessons from my dad. Be the best you can be. Never, ever give up. I see so many people who are just plain soft. There's no excuse for that. Nothing is too hard. We've got to go all the way. Nothing's going to stop us. I see that in my dad even today. He is unstoppable. He is pulled in every direction at the same time, but he keeps on going. He's a die-hard. He's amazing.

My dad is my dearest friend on earth. Our friendship is truly remarkable. I am sixty-two years old, and I talk to him almost every day. I'm amazed at what God has done with his life. Much has happened since the events at the jail in Brandon. There were forces that tried to take him out way back then, but he's now eighty-nine years old. He has received sixteen honorary doctorates and has written many books. He continues to receive accolades and awards for his tireless efforts in Christian community development and preaching God's concern for the poor.

When my dad came back from Ohio a few days ago, I told him, "I don't care how late it is when you get back, I need for you to call me, and I'll be at your house so we can talk." He was really tired, but he did that; and we talked into the late night hours.

My dad is my hero, my mentor, my friend. He has given of himself, often putting his own life at great risk for the greater good of others. He's that kind of friend. His fearless leadership has been a blessing to our family, to the boys and girls, men and women of Simpson County, the state of Mississippi, and to our great country.

Thank you, Daddy, for being a friend.

Your son, Phillip

*Phillip Perkins is a producer and songwriter; he makes his home in Jackson, Mississippi.*

# Conclusion

More than anything I want this book to serve as a discipleship tool to help us all put the Christian life into practice. God calls us to lifelong discipleship that will serve to light the way for those who are lost.

This world can be a lonely place. And when I see what is happening today—with all the division, strife, and anger—my heart aches. We've lost our way and we are tearing away at the fabric of our society. People seem to be choosing sides and not many are willing to reach across and try to fix what is broken. Friendship fills the ache in our souls and it breaks through the barriers that separate us from one another.

We began this journey by looking at the first person who God called "friend," and we asked, "What did Abraham find when he found God?" Abraham found the God of grace, and he discovered that faith brings us into His grace. He found a Friend. Moses found God to be a Friend who reveals Himself to us, and wants us to know Him as holy. David found a Friend who forgives even the worst of sinners.

When Jesus, the God-man, broke into history, finally we were able to touch Him, to see Him, to walk with Him. What the apostles found in Christ was what the Old Testament heroes found in God: they found a Friend. I love how John wrote about it. The great truth of the gospel is that He came to save us from our sins and to give us the enjoyment of fellowship with one another.

This is the message we have heard from him and declare to you: God is light; in him there is no darkness at all. If we claim to have fellowship with him and yet walk in the darkness, we lie and do not live out the truth. But if we walk in the light, as he is in the light, we have fellowship with one another, and the blood of Jesus, his Son, purifies us from all sin.—1 John 1:5–7

The joy we each have, if we are friends with God, is that we can walk in the light of His truth and draw many others to Him.

The question of the human soul is this: Who is God? And what does He want with me? I believe that God reveals Himself and His presence in the time of need. When we come to the end of ourselves, at our point of need, there we will find God. In the Old Testament they gave names to God based on how He responded in times of need. To Hagar He was *El Roi,* "the God who sees me." In her despair she ran to escape from Sarah, but God chased after her and helped her to know that He saw her and still had a plan for her (see Gen. 16:13). We read in Genesis 22:14 of how Abraham called Him *Jehovah Jireh:* The LORD Will Provide, after God provided a ram in the bush to prevent him from sacrificing his son Isaac. Moses called Him *Jehovah Nissi,* The Lord is My Banner, because when the Amalekites came upon the people of Israel to destroy them, God was their protector (Ex. 17:15). An old preacher used to say, "He's water in dry places, He's a doctor in the sick room, He's a lawyer in the courtroom, He's bread in a starving land." That's who He is. All of that and so much more.

And what God produces in us is what He wants from us. God is a Spirit, and He works through us by the Holy Spirit. I've heard people say, "The Spirit spoke to me. He said that He wants me to have a bigger house. He wants me to have a fancy this and a better that." I don't think the Spirit talks like that. I think He's saying things like, "Go to work, get yourself a job, and buy your own stuff." When the Spirit speaks, He's going to tell us something that's in His commandments. He's going to tell us something about how to use the gifts He gave us. He's going to talk to us about humility. If we are walking in Him, we are on our knees. We humble ourselves. We pull off our shoes, because we understand that we are in His presence.

I'm still learning about this humility thing. I can't have a puffed-up mind. Even when I'm seeking after God—God is the one doing it. I'm struggling between self-will and God's will. *Can I walk with You, God? Can I long for You to sit with me? Can I be content to meditate on You day and night?*

When people ask me, what do we need to do, I say there's not a list of things that you can check off one by one. It's an attitude of the heart. It's humility, and I can't quite get there on my own. God has to bring me there. The woman with the issue of blood who was making her way through the crowd trying to just touch the hem of His garment (see Luke 8:40–47). That's humility. The cry of blind Bartimaeus. That's humility. God hears every one of these feeble cries. His heart is tuned to our feeble cries because they express our desperate need for Him. Our prayer should fall in line with the prayer of William Barclay: "O Father, give us the humility which realizes its ignorance, admits its mistakes, recognizes its need, welcomes advice, accepts rebuke. Help us always to praise rather than to criticize, to sympathize rather than to condemn, to encourage rather than discourage, to build rather than to destroy, and to think of people at their best rather than at their worst."[1]

This is the secret that the powers of darkness want to keep hidden from us. They have made the smell of money, possessions, and power so strong in order to distract us from this one truth. The aroma of humility that surrounds us when we allow Him to have His way with us is what draws others. And from that place of complete humility we extend our hand to others and welcome them into the circle of our friendship with God. This circle is intended to grow as He uses us to draw others in. The size of our circle is only limited by our willingness to call others in to be warmed by His presence.

In my mind I see myself as the poor man who shared his coarse bread and tended the furnace. He wanted nothing more than to spend time with the Shah of Abbas daily. Oh, how I look forward to my time with Him every day. But I want to bring others into that circle of fellowship so they can be healed by His embrace and set free by His friendship. In all of my years of teaching—longing and hoping and dreaming that God would be present with us—there's a sense of bonding with friends that you don't have anything to do with. It's God's work.

When I look back over my life, I see Norman Nathan, Roy Rogers, Malcolm Street, and Roland Hinz in my circle. I see Kirt Lamb, Jack MacMillan, and Bob DeMoss in my circle. I see Bill Hoehm and Howard Ahmanson and so many others that are too numerous to name. God has been good to me, by enlarging my circle of friends. It's a circle that can grow each and every day. I want my circle to be multicolored. I want every ethnicity under heaven to be in my circle. I want people who used to practice every known religion in the world to be in my circle. I want people who represent every class known to humanity to be in my circle. I want God to use me to bring them into His circle of friendship and love. In the words of an old country song, the circle will "be unbroken, by and by, Lord by and by. There's a better home waiting, in the sky Lord, in the sky."

I do yearn for that home in the sky. My mother is waiting there. She's been waiting almost all of my life for me. My grandmother, my first friend, is waiting. And we are all looking forward to that day when there will be a new heaven and a new earth. The God who is our Friend will rule! And we will worship Him throughout eternity!

> Then I saw "a new heaven and a new earth," for the first heaven and the first earth had passed away, and there was no longer any sea. I saw the Holy City, the new Jerusalem, coming down out of heaven from God, prepared as a bride beautifully dressed for her husband. And I heard a loud voice from the throne saying, "Look! God's dwelling place is now among the people, and he will dwell with them. They will be his people, and God himself will be with them and be their God." —Revelation 21:1–3

We will finally come to the end of our need for God as a sin bearer. Sin will be no more. The first earth will fade away. There will be no more seas. There will be no more division. There will be circles of friends united together as one, to worship and praise the One who died and rose again to provide access for sinful man to holy God. We will finally see Him, in all of His glory—we will see Him . . . face-to-face . . . and the song of my soul will be this:

> Amazing grace! how sweet the sound,
>   That saved a wretch; like me!
> I once was lost, but now am found,
>   Was blind, but now I see.
>
>       .   .   .   .   .   .   .   .   .
>
> When we've been there ten thousand years,
>   Bright shining as the sun,
> We've no less days to sing God's praise
>   Than when we first begun.[2]

It is His amazing grace that saved me from my sins, and gave me friends who picked me up when I was falling. And in the end we will all be together . . . friends of every color, every creed, every class . . . with arms lifted high in praise and thanksgiving to Jesus. All eyes will be fixed on Him. He is the One who came to live among us. He is the One who died for our sins. He is the Author and the Finisher of our faith. He is the One who made heaven possible for us. And every one of us will be able to say with great joy—*He Calls Me Friend*!

# To Think About and Talk Over

## Chapter 1: The Hound of Heaven Who Pursues

1. We learn from Abraham that God pursues us for friendship and relationship. How have you felt His pursuit in your life, both before and after conversion?
2. Dr. Perkins struggled to believe that God could really be his friend. What is your view of God? How has this chapter impacted how you see Him?
3. God makes and keeps His promises. Why is this important? What is the promise that means the most to you? Explain.
4. Abraham gave up everything in pursuit of friendship with God. Have you given up everything, or are you still holding on to things that interfere with your friendship with God? What are those things that are standing in the way of full devotion to Him?

## Chapter 2: The Intimate, Holy One

1. The poor man wanted nothing more than to share his heart with the Shah of Abbas—no gift could compare to that. Does this describe your attitude about time with God? Why or why not?
2. The story of Moses allows us to see how God was working behind the scenes to prepare him for His purposes. How has He directed your life to prepare you for what He has called you to do?

3. What does it mean to you that God wants you to know Him? How would you characterize your knowledge of Him right now? What are you motivated to do to know Him better?

## Chapter 3: The Great Forgiver

1. David said that all sin is against God. Do you agree with this? Why or why not?

2. David did some pretty awful things: lust, adultery, deceit, murder—yet God forgave him. How does that speak to you with respect to the sin you commit? How can this truth serve as a bridge to reach those who need to know God as friend?

3. "When someone hurts us we should write it down in the sand where the winds of forgiveness can erase it away. But when someone does something good for us, we must engrave it in stone where no wind can ever erase it." How closely does this reflect your attitude and response toward how others treat you?

## Chapter 4: The God Who Came to Us

1. Dr. Perkins suggests that friendship with God requires humility; that we "stay low." What does that mean in a very practical way to you as you approach and interact with potential new friends?

2. What does it mean to you that He will carry your burdens? How can this truth help us to connect with others, especially those who are hurting?

3. Jesus modeled intentional friendship for us. He shared His heart, spent time, and made the ultimate sacrifice for His friends. Who are you intentional about being a

friend with, and how have those friendships developed over time?

## Chapter 5: Friend of Prostitutes, Thieves, and the Outsider

1. Jesus befriended the outcasts of His day. Who are the people who fit into this category today? When you think of befriending them, how much control does fear have over you? How can fear of God cast out your fear of people?
2. Do you live a life that is isolated from unbelievers? What can you change that will bring you in close contact with them regularly?
3. How comfortable are you in crossing class and racial barriers to form friendships? What aspect of these potential friendships makes you uncomfortable? Are there persons that the Holy Spirit is prompting you to go a little further with?

## Chapter 6: The God Who Dwells Within

1. Dr. Perkins describes the tugging of the Holy Spirit and says that He uses circumstances in our lives to cause us to cry out to God and to seek His will and His purposes. How aware are you of the Holy Spirit directing your life?
2. One of the first clear acts of the Holy Spirit was reconciling the Jews with Gentiles—people they previously saw as unclean. How is He moving you to reconcile with people who are different from you?
3. The Holy Spirit came in a bold way, and He gave boldness to the early Christians to talk about Jesus. Are there opportunities that you have missed to boldly

speak for Him? Share about them and pray together for boldness at the next opportunity.

## Chapter 7: The Fruit of Friendship

1. How aware are you of the battle between two wolves that is raging inside? Which wolf have you been feeding? How have you been feeding it? Are there changes that He would have you make?
2. If we are known by the fruit we produce, what type of fruit do the persons who know you best see?
3. The fruit of the Spirit is love, joy, peace, forbearance, kindness, goodness, faithfulness, gentleness, and self-control. Which of these is most lacking in your life? Pray together that the Holy Spirit would fully develop this aspect of His character in your life.

## Chapter 8: Crossing Hard Lines

1. Dr. Perkins suggests that friendship always begins with the other person, and an understanding of what his or her needs are. How can service to others who are outside your normal circle of friends help you get started?
2. What does Dr. Perkins's friendship with Tommy Tarrants teach you about crossing color lines? What do you believe about friendship across color lines?
3. Dr. Perkins benefited from great friends who were mentors in his life. They had wisdom about life that they poured into him. What opportunities for mentoring or being mentored is the Holy Spirit directing you to?

## Chapter 9: The Friendship Challenge

1. How would you define the good life? Who are the persons that you know who need this? Pray for

opportunities to help them know and experience God.

2. Friendship pursues, goes deep, forgives, crosses lines, is "with," and bears fruit. Which aspect is most challenging for you? Share why. Ask the Holy Spirit to develop you in this area.

3. If you were to die tonight, consider the size of your friendship circle—how many of them know Jesus as Savior? Do they all look alike? Are they all from the same social class? How would He desire your circle to grow before you see Him face-to-face? Every day is an opportunity to grow this circle until our very last breath.

**Into Life:** Dr. Perkins has mentioned a number of his special friends throughout this book. Make a list of your circle of friends.

- *How many of them are friends of Jesus?* Pray regularly that they would each begin to reach across lines to befriend others and bring them into the circle.
- *How many of them are not yet friends of Jesus?* Pray regularly for them to find the joy and peace in knowing Him as friend.

# NOTES

## Introduction

1. E. J. Dionne, Jr.,"Is America Getting Lonelier?," *Washington Post*, August 6, 2017, https://www.washingtonpost.com/opinions/is-america-getting-lonelier/2017/08/06/411522a6-7933-11e7-8f39-eeb7d3a2d304_story.html.
2. Natasha Bach, "'One of the Greatest Public Health Challenges of Our Time.' The U.K. Just Rolled Out Its Plan for Fighting Loneliness,"*Fortune Magazine*, October 15, 2018, http://fortune.com/2018/10/15/uk-government-loneliness-strategy/.
3. Ibid.
4. David Frank, "1 in 3 US Adults are Lonely, Survey Shows," *AARP*, September 26, 2018, https://www.aarp.org/home-family/friends-family/info-2018/loneliness-survey.html.
5. George Will, "How Do We Heal the Epidemic of Loneliness?," *Washington Post*, October 14, 2018, https://tylerpaper.com/opinion/columnists/how-do-we-heal-the-epidemic-of-loneliness/article_c03d52c6-cd90-11e8-8eb2-bb29b7a6f3f6.html.
6. J. Langford, "Friendship," D. Mangum, D. R. Brown, R. Klippenstein, and R. Hurst, eds, *Lexham Theological Wordbook* (Bellingham, WA: Lexham Press, 2014).
7. Galen C. Dalrymple, "The Meaning of Friend," Daybreak Devotions.com, April 28, 2015, https://daybreaksdevotions.wordpress.com/2015/04/28/daybreaks-for-42815-the-meaning-of-friend/.
8. James Weldon Johnson, "The Creation," Poets.org, 1945, https://www.poets.org/poetsorg/poem/creation.
9. Bill Thrasher, *Living the Life God Has Planned* (Chicago: Moody, 2001), 18–19.
10. Megan Carlier, Timothy Crouch, Avery Johnson, study group notes: "He Called Me Friend Draft Introduction," March 15, 2019.

## Chapter One: The Hound of Heaven Who Pursues

1. Melissa Harris, "Executive Profile: Martin Nesbitt, the first friend," *Chicago Tribune*, January 21, 2013, https://www.chicagotribune.com/business/ct-xpm-2013-01-21-ct-biz-0121-executive-profile-nesbitt-20130121-story.html.
2. John Perkins and Wayne Gordon, *Leadership Revolution* (Ventura, CA: Regal Books, 2012), 183.
3. Russell Carter, "Standing on the Promises," Timeless Truths, https://library.timelesstruths.org/music/Standing_on_the_Promises/.
4. Roger Rosenblatt, "John Glenn: A Realm Where Age Doesn't Count," *Time*, August 17, 1998.
5. "How old was Isaac when Abraham almost sacrificed him?," Got Questions, https://www.gotquestions.org/how-old-was-Isaac.html.
6. A. W. Tozer, *Three Spiritual Classics in One Volume* (Chicago: Moody, 2018), 356.
7. Ruth Gledhill, "'I Miss My father, But He Gave His Life for Christ': Daughter of Murdered Missionary Jim Elliot Speaks Out," *Christianity Today*, February

23, 2017, https://www.christiantoday.com/article/i-miss-my-father-but-he-gave-his-life-for-christ-daughter-of-murdered-christian-missionary-speaks-out/104967.html.

8. Stephen E. Berk, *A Time to Heal: John Perkins, Community Development and Racial Reconciliation* (Grand Rapids: Baker Books, 1997), 93.

9. Tozer, *Three Spiritual Classics in One Volume*, 228.

## Chapter Two: The Intimate, Holy One

1. A. Naismith in Paul Lee Tan, "Signs of the Times," *Encyclopedia of 7700 Illustrations* (Garland, TX: Bible Communications, Inc., 1996), 904.

2. If you'd like to read about Abraham's great-grandson Joseph and how the Israelites ended up in Egypt, see Genesis chapters 37; 39–48; 50.

3. "Ordinary People," written by James Cleveland, 1978.

4. Bob Smietana, "LifeWay Research: Americans are Fond of the Bible, Don't Actually Read It," LifeWay Research, April 25, 2017, https://lifewayresearch.com/2017/04/25/lifeway-research-americans-are-fond-of-the-bible-dont-actually-read-it/.

5. Reginald Heber, "Holy, Holy, Holy," Timeless Truths, https://library.timelesstruths.org/music/Holy_Holy_Holy/.

6. A. T. Pierson, "The Eagle," in Joseph S. Exell, *The Biblical Illustrator* (Grand Rapids: Baker Publishing Group, 1978), 1905-09.

7. Colin Powell Quotes, Good Reads, https://www.goodreads.com/quotes/310930-the-less-you-associate-with-some-people-the-more-your-life-will-improve.

8. You can read about this special event at http://oneracemovement.com/onerace-stone-mountain/ and at https://stream.org/stone-mountain-one-race-christian-unity/.

9. Phillip Perkins, "He Calls Me Friend," written and copyrighted 2019.

## Chapter Three: The Great Forgiver

1. "Having a Best Friend," Sermon Central, https://www.sermoncentral.com/sermon-illustrations/11937/two-friends-were-walking-through-the-desert-by-johanna-radelfinger.

2. Andraé Crouch, "Take Me Back," copyright ©1973 Bud John Songs (ASCAP) (adm. at CapitolCMGPublishing.com). All rights reserved. Used by permission.

3. William Barclay, *The Gospel of Luke*, quoted in Charles Swindoll, *The Tale of the Tardy Oxcart and 1501 Other Stories: "Forgiveness"* (Nashville: Word Publishing, 1998), 216–17.

4. Henri Nouwen, "Receiving Forgiveness," Henri Nouwen Society, Daily E-Meditation, January 25, 2019, https://henrinouwen.org/meditation/receiving-forgiveness/.

5. "I die daily," 1 Corinthians 15:31 in the New American Standard Bible.

6. Bruce Larson, *Setting Men Free*, quoted in Swindoll, *The Tale of the Tardy Oxcart*, 214.

## Chapter Four: The God Who Came to Us

1. Paul Harvey, "Incarnation," in Swindoll, *The Tale of the Tardy Oxcart*, 294–95.

2. Andrew Murray, "Humility is," quoted in Paul Tan, *Encyclopedia of 7700 Illustrations* (Pittsburgh: Assurance Publishers, 1990), 2304.

3. Tony Evans, *Tony Evans' Book of Illustrations* (Chicago: Moody, 2009), 158.
4. Joseph M. Scriven, "What a Friend We Have in Jesus," Hymnal.net, https://www.hymnal.net/en/hymn/h/789.
5. John Perkins and Wayne Gordon, *Leadership Revolution* (Ventura, CA: Regal Publishing, 2012), 64.
6. John Perkins, *One Blood: Parting Words to the Church on Race and Love* (Chicago: Moody Publishers, 2018), 164–65.
7. Don Richardson, "Peace Child," quoted in Tan, *Encyclopedia of 7700 Illustrations*, 1185.
8. George C. Hugg, Johnson Oatman Jr., "No, Not One," Hymnal.net, https://www.hymnal.net/en/hymn/h/992.

### Chapter Five: Friend of Prostitutes, Thieves, and the Outsider

1. Kimi Harris, "Jesus Befriended Prostitutes. So This Victorian-Era Woman Did Too," *Christianity Today*: Christian History, July 15, 2018, https://www.christianitytoday.com/history/channel/utilities/print.html?type=article&id=142851.
2. Perkins and Gordon, *Leadership Revolution*, 45.
3. Tim Keller, Twitter post, December 10, 2018, 3:37 p.m., https://twitter.com/timkellernyc/status/1072274184867377153?lang=en.

### Chapter Six: The God Who Dwells Within

1. Illustrations Unlimited: "He Felt God Tugging on His Heart," Ministry 127, http://ministry127.com/resources/illustration/he-felt-god-tugging-on-his-heart.
2. Millard J. Erickson, *Christian Theology* (Grand Rapids: Baker Academic, 1998), 771.
3. James Merritt and John P. Jewell, "Spiritual Thirst," Bible Center, https://www.biblecenter.com/sermons/spiritualthirst.htm.
4. Sarah Eekhoff Zylstra, "The Final Call of John Perkins," The Gospel Coalition, April 2, 2018, https://www.thegospelcoalition.org/article/final-charge-john-m-perkins/.
5. Erwin Lutzer, "God Owns Our Tongues," Moody Church Media, 2005, https://www.moodymedia.org/articles/god-owns-our-tongues/.
6. Mark Galli and Ted Olsen, eds., "Polycarp: Aged Bishop of Smyrna," *131 Christians Everyone Should Know* (Nashville: Broadman & Holman, 2000), 360.
7. Ludie Carrington Day Pickett, "I've Seen the Lightning Flashing," Hymnal.net, https://www.hymnal.net/en/hymn/h/688.

### Chapter Seven: The Fruit of Friendship

1. Jamie Buckingham, *Power for Living*, 1999, http://www.sermonillustrations.com/a-z/f/father.htm.
2. Wayne Parker, "Statistics on Fatherless Children in America," LiveAbout, https://www.liveabout.com/fatherless-children-in-america-statistics-1270392.
3. Daniel Henderson, *The Deeper Life: Satisfying the 8 Vital Longings of Your Soul* (Minneapolis: Bethany House, 2014), 37.
4. Kali Hawlk, "Do You Feed the Good Wolf or the Bad Wolf?," *Huffington Post*, August 27, 2015, https://www.huffingtonpost.com/kali-hawlk/do-you-feed-the-good-wolf_b_8048124.html.

5. Walter A. Elwell, "Peace," in *Baker Encyclopedia of the Bible*, vol. 2, ed. Walter A. Elwell (Grand Rapids: Baker, 1988), 1634.
6. William Gurnall, *Daily Readings from The Christian in Complete Armour* (Chicago: Moody, 1994), September 11 entry, "Division Among Brethren."
7. "pistis: faith, faithfulness," *Strong's Concordance*, Bible Hub, https://biblehub.com/greek/4102.htm.
8. J. Oswald Sanders, *Spiritual Leadership* (Chicago: Moody, 2017), 74.
9. "Self-control (*egkrateia*)," *Strong's Concordance*, Bible Hub, https://biblehub.com/greek/1466.htm.
10. Nathan Johnson, "Someone Stronger," November 13, 2009, Sermon Central, https://www.sermoncentral.com/sermon-illustrations/74286/d-l-moody-illustrates-how-to-grow-by-sermoncentral.
11. Bill Bright, "The Steps to Being Filled with the Holy Spirit," Cru, https://www.cru.org/us/en/train-and-grow/transferable-concepts/be-filled-with-the-holy-spirit.7.html.
12. Craig Brian Larson, *750 Engaging Illustrations for Preachers, Teachers, and Writers* (Grand Rapids: Baker Publishing, 2002).

### Chapter Eight: Crossing Hard Lines

1. "Project Empathy Works to Combat Homelessness with Humanity, Personal Touch," Fox 13, August 6, 2018, https://fox13now.com/2018/08/06/project-empathy-works-to-combat-homelessness-with-humanity-personal-touch/.
2. "CCD Philosophy," Christian Community Development Association, https://ccda.org/about/philosophy/.
3. Jerry Mitchell, *The Preacher and the Klansman* (Jackson, MS: The Clarion Ledger, 1999), 53.
4. Ibid.
5. John Perkins, Thomas A. Tarrants III, *He's My Brother: Former Racial Foes Offer Strategy for Reconciliation* (Grand Rapids: Baker, 1994).
6. G. C. Jones, *1000 Illustrations for Preaching and Teaching* (Nashville: Broadman & Holman Publishers, 1986), 186.

### Chapter Nine: The Friendship Challenge

1. Samantha Boardman, M.D., "Why We Love Talking About Ourselves," *Psychology Today*, March 7, 2017, https://www.psychologytoday.com/us/blog/positive-prescription/201703/why-we-love-talking-about-ourselves.
2. Belinda Luscombe, "Why We Talk about Ourselves: The Brain Likes It," *Time*, http://healthland.time.com/2012/05/08/why-we-overshare-the-brain-likes-it/.
3. Shauna Niequist, *Bittersweet: Thoughts on Change, Grace, and Learning the Hard Way* (Grand Rapids: Zondervan, 2010), 32.
4. "About," Christian Community Development Association, https://ccda.org/about/.
5. Hubert H. Humphrey, *Wit & Wisdom of Hubert H. Humphrey* (Oaks, PA: Partners Press, 1984).

### Conclusion

1. Kurt Bjorklund, *Prayers for Today* (Chicago: Moody, 2011), 65.
2. John Newton, "Amazing Grace," Hymnal.net, https://www.hymnal.net/en/hymn/h/313.

# ACKNOWLEDGMENTS

I am above grateful for the people who have graced my life as friends. There truly is not enough space in this book to talk about all of them. To say thank you for their investment of time and talents that have fed my soul and have made me what I am. I am eternally grateful for . . .

—Those personal friends who took the time to write a special contribution for this book: Ken, Randy and Joan, Wayne, and my son Phillip. Thank you for sharing the stories of our friendship.

—Megan Carlier, Timothy Crouch, and Avery Johnson. Your excitement for this project almost outran my own! I'm grateful for you.

—The Moody Publishers family. To you, Duane, for seeing the vision even as the Lord was giving it to me. And to you, Karen, for helping me share a message that is so close to my heart. This has been another labor of love. May the Lord make much of the work of our hands.

# WORDS OF WISDOM TO THE NEXT GENERATION FROM A PIONEER OF THE CIVIL RIGHTS MOVEMENT

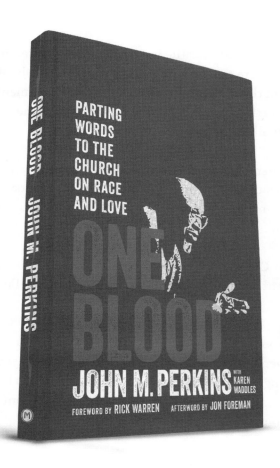

MOODY
Publishers®

*From the Word to Life®*

In this his crowning work, Dr. Perkins speaks honestly to the church about—in his own words—"the things I've discovered to be crucial about reconciliation, discipleship, and justice... the principles I believe to be vital to a complete ministry of reconciliation." Here is a final manifesto from a man whose life's work has been reconciliation.

978-0-8024-1801-2  |  also available as an eBook

Study me, observe my grace, and explore my cultured beauty.
I dare you to reveal what exists behind my dark brown eyes;
Reproduction of many archetypes.
Nevertheless, leading with direction in a bid to follow what I desire.
Allow me to teach you my essence,
While society draws and manipulates me into
Its visualized perfection.
I have outlined and developed the strong point of artistry
From every angle of collaged damage.
I communicate through abstracts as it conveys
Information about who I am.
Do not define me without lessons.
I have molded myself into a balanced painter.
I am the center,
I am an art,
And never will I visit the day where my harmonious
Features become levied.

**Depiction**

Anger has consumed what was left of Eden.
It has controlled every decision brought to pass.
My emotions respond to the world with indignation, being
Motivated by a lower level of depression.
I beg the universe,
*"Allow me to be sad, as rage seems to last."*
Misery is draped around my soul and luring the light.
I dread the days when the sun is upright.
She follows my sinfully barren life.
My depression teases me by finessing hope.
When the stars shine bright,
I escape to the shadows, romanticizing a tight-rope.
I mourn for the woman, counting her tears.
With little sense of reality,
Their smiles appear effortlessly,
As I am in the midst of their tenderness with a frown.

**The Magnitude of Anger**

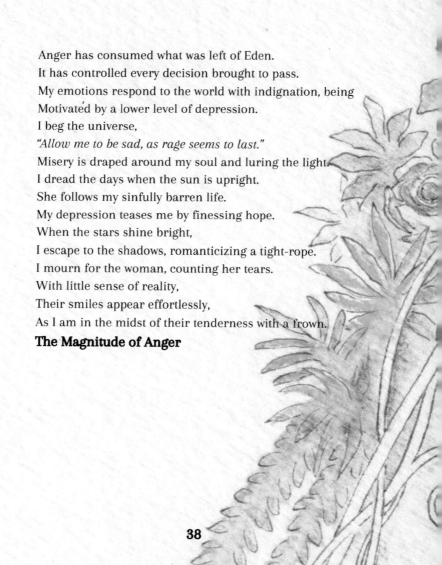

Insecurities spewed down my throat and were choked on.
Those hard-to-swallow words were distasteful, unpleasantly
Resting in the pit of my stomach.
I loathed self-doubt while the threat of him pursuing a younger
Woman tormented my self-esteem.
The reconstruction of many shortcomings had begun.
Strength was inherited from the grief endured,
Knocking down every obstacle in my way, and being
Mindful of the importance of joy.
The ball and chain wrapped around my ankles were removed,
Then I had the strength to walk away.
The weapons formed against me were stored on a shelf as a
Reminder that he did not prosper.

**Reclassifying my Worth**

40

There was a time I meditated and excavated through
The depth of who I am.
Searching for purpose; she did not want to be found.
Happiness was once reflected as a hopeless emotion.
The cloaked feelings hid sullenly, pulling me into Satan's mist,
Relying on his comfort as he vested losses in my life.
I took the air for miles, barefooted, on an abandoned
Road, and drained of self-control.
All while chasing heaven for an end,
Until I ran into faith and was forced to feel my way
Through the pain.
Crying in the sun felt good.
My trembling body felt lighter.
My harmful mood felt brighter.
I wrote off subjection,
Convincing myself that I mattered.
My soul has yet to be neglected by hell's fence.
She has been shining since.

**Soul Shining**

Thrive for you.
Live for you.
Travel the earth to find meaning for you.
Leverage my soul for you.
Manifest what belongs to you.
With every breath I take, it belongs to you.

**I Love Myself**

She was defiant but ornery.
Natural but flattering.
Pocket-book full of blues, preparing herself for the next bruise.
To him, she was colorless,
A bloodless mistress in dirty linen, accepting remission of sin,
Just to do it again.
His commandments are honeyed after
Releasing into her broken walls.
Pieces of her identity fade.
She drifts, surrendering to a light that flickers at
The speed of her heartbeat.
If she takes just enough, the anxieties of being
Hopeless will be swept away.
The clouds will be her cushion.

**Blue Heaven**

44

I write my name on his back with oil,
Marking my territory,
Afraid to lose him, but the greatest fear is losing
The connection that keeps him close.
We protect our feelings for one another.
Committed to preserving the romance, our
Enemy curses through their night's affliction.
Giving up my heart with no expectations,
I thrive off pleasing him.
The belly of my mind has conceived his thoughts
And like the wind knows the purpose of its breeze,
I know the meaning of his wants and needs.
He whispers in my ear, and I am aroused.
The obsession of bearing his sons
Overwhelms my womb.
With permission, he grasps my waist, initiating
An out-of-body intimacy.
My eyes redressed the ceiling
Into meaningful colors,
And the room filled with red heat.
Ties of the soul have a whole new meaning.
Lovemaking is underrated.
I have gravitated and levitated into a world filled
With sexual motivations.

**Mind, Body, and Soul**

May I heal you with my words?
Proverbs are escaping from the darkness of my mouth,
Just to reach the restless depths of the pain that
Intercepts your strength to live.
Your emotional debts have isolated you in misery,
Swaying others to be your company.
My fragile friend, I pray to the sky that you find more
Reasons to survive.
You avoid a handful of tears by inhaling hate and
Exhaling unclaimed hurt.
Your breath has become toxic.
Let us heal the wounds that scar but never disappear.
Take time to save who you are meant to be rather than
Your present entity.
Know you are strong in the ground, a compassionate
Woman destined to stick around.

**Healing With Words**

He rages and I am to blame for the rapid storms
Destroying his foundation.
I frown upon a man's inability to renovate
The home he destroyed.
My own people try to triumph over the ambitions instilled
Inside of me, refusing to see how
Perpetual and relentless I can be.
I lie low once I scintillate through the skies with grace,
Elevated, and surpassing everyone's safe space.
Expect greatness from the woman who chooses to never be
Comfortable with complacency.
Her heavenly expectancy will never be on good terms
With hellish tendencies.
That woman is me.
Nature called, and I answered with an aligned spirit.
A village of angels sends me flowers, gifting me to be the Maker of all.
Now the people will bow down to my infinite vine as an
Omen of my wrath.

**Earth's Goddess**

Stem winding.
Soul-stirring,
Mind-bending masterpiece.
The epitome of delicacy.
**Human Rose**

I perished in a quilted wrapper after
Falling short of mental hygiene,
Decided to speed through life without tying my shoestrings.
My mind documented weak thoughts followed by destruction,
Conceiving a war that I was too frail to fight in.
The deep red-colored waves of my silent
Sea had no ability to flow steadily.
Like a seahorse, my value became unrecognized.
I modeled a shy creature dying quietly.
Planted inside of a woman to be born strong but raised weak,
And the day fear stroked my tongue,
My silence kept me safe.
This unstable heart would beat with every tragedy,
And I felt it failing as I chose to be eaten by the world's demons.
A harp played in harmony,
Confessing why life miscarried me and how I became nameless.
Did they recognize my song of sorrow?
I surrendered fully and the waters around me has dried up.
The flowers has ceased their bloom.
Wisdom I have been granted.
The last number has become known.
My flesh no longer kneels for
Validation and my spirit thrives.

**Final Waters**

The wind howls at your strength,
As you push through the storms.
The wave of life surrounds you with vices
And you are hit at full speed.
We'll never see the affliction of travail.
Your scars envy your soul.
The ravages want to be a part of your growth,
But you refuse to let it show.
When I stare as you pass by
It is not to dwell,
I can just tell that you wear your pain so well.

**Survivor**

The sounds of the flowing Neuse River are faint with nature.
I run past hardy bushes; my nose kisses the jasmine-scented
Honeysuckles until nightfall.
The dark Carolina sky is brightened by fireflies.
I remember sitting in the back of my mother's car,
Wishing upon many stars.
And right before the streetlights lit twice,
I ride on a bike with worn-out tires,
Collecting dirt and skipping rocks as I go faster.
My hands and body greet the air while standing on the pedals.
It feels good to be alone, to have no one in sight;
The type of freedom that a child feels for only a fleeting time.
Take back the worldly strife.
Give me back my adolescent life.

**A Kid Again**

My crown tilts as voices sway with negativity;
Only with permission will you see my vulnerability.
I have rigged my emotions for the sake of losing myself.
The aesthetics of my exterior are precious, a level of
Pretty nature that cannot be seen.
My confidence has empowered me to heal.
Words cannot violate the thickness of my skin.
Perceptions will never determine the beauty I have
Refined from within.

**My Beauty**

You are stuck saving hate for your bloodline.
Selfishly pleading to your conscious,
*"Never involve yourself with oppression.*
*It does not belong to you."*
You have witnessed death,
There's no remorse for the bindingly bleak ones.
Aloofness elongates division and separation.
Your "Just Be Kind" signed on your
Front lawn only applies to the people who sit in the
Box with you.
**Boxed Up Hate**

A wanderer, but I am not rootless.
Venturing to the source of my river, and with no hesitation,
I walk into the waters of hope.
As it gently covers my undisguised skin, the truth seeps
Through the pores of my foundation,
Restoring what has been fragmented by the
Seduction of impurity.
Before leaving trails of the polluted past,
I stop to see beauty in the reflection of my water streams.
I am grace,
I am no longer weeping over the debt that has burdened my Existence with
insecurities.
I am sound.
The illusion of ego does not consume my spirit.
I am selfless.
I do not compete; the strange ground
I walk on knows who I am.
My ancestors' blood seeps through the soil,
So, I walk, respecting every step I take.
I am divinely collecting knowledge that was left behind.
A crown is just an object that has been taken from me.
I am a queen without it.
I learned to love before I could eat.
There is nothing one can take from my serenity.
I am at Peace.
**Clarity**

## ABOUT THE AUTHOR

Courtney Holmes was born in a small town called Smithfield, North Carolina, where she grew up enjoying community get togethers in the park and dancing to Kirk Franklin "Stomp" every year. North Carolina will always be a place that taught her the love for community. When she was eleven years old, her stepfather joined the military and all the places they had lived taught her the meaning of diversity. Courtney's love for reading and writing lead her into her journey of writing poetry. She writes best at four in the morning. Yes, she is the most creative in the morning but that is her only down time as she then spends the rest of the day chasing three toddlers. Courtney Holmes loves spending her free time at open mic nights expressing her love for poetry through spoken word and craft beer. Ms. Holmes and her family call the Texas area home.

Share your thoughts!
www.courtneyholmes.org
Instagram: @starfiretheversier

# ACKNOWLEDGEMENT

To Naomi, Nathanael, and Noah the three little people with
limited words, who has motivated me to continue
following my dreams by simply existing. Special thanks to
Richie Marrufo the host of Barbed Wire Open Mic Series.
You have given artists like me a platform, I am grateful. To
the many friends and family with their continued
encouragement...Thank you.